DIFFERENCE NOT DISORDER

of related interest

Medical Aspects of Autism and Asperger Syndrome
A Guide for Parents and Professionals
Mohammad Ghaziuddin
ISBN 978 1 84310 818 4
eISBN 978 1 78450 783 1

The Interbrain
Embodied Connections Versus Common Knowledge
Dibgy Tantam
ISBN 978 1 84905 476 8
eISBN 978 0 85700 856 5

A Best Practice Guide to Assessment and Intervention for Autism Spectrum Disorder in Schools, Second Edition
Lee A. Wilkinson
ISBN 978 1 78592 704 1
eISBN 978 1 78450 250 8

Creating Autism Champions
Autism Awareness Training for Key Stage 1 and 2
Joy Beaney
Illustrated by Haitham Al-Ghani
ISBN 978 1 78592 169 8
eISBN 978 1 78450 441 0

A Practical Guide to Happiness in Children and Teens on the Autism Spectrum
A Positive Psychology Approach
Victoria Honeybourne
ISBN 978 1 78592 347 0
eISBN 978 1 78450 681 0

The Essential Manual for Asperger Syndrome (ASD) in the Classroom
What Every Teacher Needs to Know
Kathy Hoopmann
Illustrated by Rebecca Houkamau
ISBN 978 1 84905 553 6
eISBN 978 0 85700 984 5

Autism and Solution-focused Practice
Els Mattelin and Hannelore Volckaert
ISBN 978 1 78592 328 9
eISBN 978 1 78450 644 5

Autism and Learning Differences
An Active Learning Teaching Toolkit
Michael P. McManmon, Ed.D.
Foreword by Stephen M. Shore
ISBN 978 1 84905 794 3
eISBN 978 1 78450 074 0

DIFFERENCE NOT DISORDER

Understanding Autism Theory in Practice

DR CATHERINE HARVEY

Illustrated by Kevin McFadden

Jessica Kingsley *Publishers*
London and Philadelphia

First published in 2018
by Jessica Kingsley Publishers
73 Collier Street
London N1 9BE, UK
and
400 Market Street, Suite 400
Philadelphia, PA 19106, USA

www.jkp.com

Library of Congress Cataloging in Publication Data
A CIP catalog record for this book is available from the Library of Congress

British Library Cataloguing in Publication Data
A CIP catalogue record for this book is available from the British Library

ISBN 978 1 78592 474 3
eISBN 978 1 78450 863 0

Printed and bound in the United States

I dedicate this book to David and Althea Brandon, without whom I would not have become either the person or the teacher I grew into. I owe them more than I can acknowledge in words – I owe them every word of this book, because without them it would never have been written. They literally saved my life by taking me home. In many ways, my life was one of their legacies. They live 'in my middle' forever.

With my undying love and gratitude.

Contents

PART II. UNDERSTANDING THE THEORY OF AUTISM AS DIFFERENCE IN PRACTICE

Preface

This book is written for all young children with autism, their parents, grandparents, carers and extended families, and the numerous professionals who work with them. It is written with love and appreciation for all the children and adults I have worked with and alongside, and with hope for those who follow in our footsteps that the knowledge and insight it offers will illuminate and better inform their paths, making them easier to walk.

Furthermore, it is underpinned by the same personal and educational values that underpinned my practice and passionately guided my professional and academic inquiries. They are the same values that led me to fight for inclusion long before it was a popular idea, and to the recognition of autism as a difference rather than a disease, long before the plethora of books, articles and stories we have today supporting this viewpoint. They also led me to the agonised admission that 'melting-pot', 'one-size-fits-all' classrooms/schools cannot work for all our children, especially those with autism; an idea argued and developed in this book.

In writing the book I have endeavoured to write each chapter as an independent entity that could be read separately to enable readers to start and finish reading where and when they wished. Also, I have tried to give my personal answers to the predominant questions asked of me throughout my years of educational practice, such as my opinions regarding the measles, mumps and rubella (MMR) controversy and the possible increase in the prevalence of autism. I do so from a viewpoint informed by my lived experience, training and study, and underpinned by my personal and educational values. In my practice, I explored the topical issues in this field, looking at them from professional and academic perspectives. However, whatever opinions I formed were guided by values and shaped by hands-on experience. They were never abstract ideas or constructions adopted without consideration and trial.

As an entirety, the book divides into two distinctive sections. In Part I, Chapters 1 to 4 provide the reader with a historical view of the theories and approaches regarding autism, exploring how we arrived at our current constructions and interventions, and delving into some of the controversial issues around these. The aims of these chapters are (1) to further understanding of the current socio-educational practice regarding children with autism through the lens of historical insights and knowledge and, from this, (2) to inspire the reader to critically evaluate concepts and approaches when reading about autism and/or deciding upon the best interventions for individual children.

I apologise for the age of some of the ideas and concepts included in Chapters 1 to 4, acknowledging that the field of autism has moved rapidly, making some earlier constructions obsolete. However, I make no apologies for their inclusion. Historical insights and theories are not merely included to inform parents and professionals new to the field of how we arrived at where we are today; they are also included because during my practice I often witnessed new methods and approaches being marketed as unique, promising new hope to parents and professionals alike. However, with my embodied history of autism and knowledge of the theories from which we were coming to better understand it, I could recognise both similarities to previous interventions and the theories underpinning the method/approach. Those new to the field did not have the advantage of this long-term perspective. Therefore, I wish to share this historical overview and the insights it gave. Significantly I do so from the point of view of a practitioner with a focus predominantly upon the constructions, interventions and outcomes for the young student/child with autism.

Meanwhile, in Part II, Chapters 5 to 8, building upon the premise introduced in Chapters 1 to 4 that autism is a different way of perceiving and relating to the external world, provide practical guidance regarding behaviours, practices and methods for caring for and educating children with autism. Significantly, all aspects of the guidance given arose from the embodied knowledge of lengthy educational practice, nourished by academic study, professional in-service training and passionate personal interest.

Also in these final chapters I explore some of the essential features needed to make schools fit to teach our children/students with autism. Again, these were developed in my practice and are the substance of academic study, professional practice and personal, socio-educational values. They are directed at we who are now called the 'neurotypicals' in the hope that we will become aware that we are living alongside those who are different, not less nor impaired. They require us to stop our grand design to normalise this difference in the great 'melting-pot' experiment we have legitimised under the emotional banner of 'inclusion' and to educate our children/students with due regard for their learning styles and needs. Ultimately, they pose the question from which Chapter 1 emerges: 'What if we got it wrong?'

Finally, throughout the book, I use the term children/person with autism rather than the term now prevalent in society, 'the autistic'. Holding the viewpoint that first we see the person/child before any state or condition of being, autism is not for me an overall descriptor of any child/person. Therefore, for me, all states or conditions of being should be sublimated to the humanity of the person/child/group we are referring to. May we all strive to put the humanity of others before their diagnosis.

PART I

AUTISM HISTORY AND THEORY

Thinking and Constructs Underpinning Autism as We Know It Today

Chapter 1

WHAT IF WE GOT IT WRONG?

Introduction

In this chapter I outline the main idea from which this book emerged, that is, in constructing autism as a disorder we may have it wrong. In doing so, I argue that this view has led to our current endeavours to fit students with autism into a socio-educational system that often stresses, distresses and confuses them, and that if we change our view to one in which autism is a 'different mind' then we could be free to provide school/classroom environments that are more fitting to these students.

Following this, I briefly outline how autism is currently constructed by those, like me, on the outside looking in. I have done this because, even with society's increased social awareness of this condition, no book on this topic can at present be written without a brief description of autism given its pervasive and behavioural-based nature.

The Book's Origin: What If We Got It Wrong?

In writing this book I am guided by two beliefs. The first is that knowledge has different forms. For example, within the field of autism we have what may be considered academic, professional and personal knowledge, that is, the contributions to knowledge made by research articles are filed under academic knowledge; the contributions to practice made by educational approaches and methods are classed as professional knowledge; and the ad hoc contributions to human insight and understanding made by anecdote and experience are considered personally acquired knowledge. However, in our science-driven world, academic and professional knowledge, which often resemble each other, have become paramount over personal or lived/embodied knowledge. For me this is a crucial, debilitating imbalance because personal knowledge often grounds or earths both academic and professional knowledge:

> Like the elements of electricity, I see the academy as the neutral, steady current and the profession as the live, pulsating one. Although electricity will flow with just these currents, it is unsafe without the earthed element of the personal. This 'earth-ing' occurs in the embodiment of knowledge within the reflective practitioner in which knowing, doing and being become one. (Harvey 2015, p.20)

The second premise guiding this book is that, regardless of the form of knowledge we draw our ideas from, our actions are guided by (1) what we value and (2) our personal constructions, and that these (3) are often bound to the cultural beliefs of our society and our generation. Therefore, if I construct that the world is governed by objective laws and truths which can be known, and once known used to predict outcomes, I will value the scientific research of academic knowledge above all other forms of knowledge. If, on the other hand, I construct that the world can only be known through subjective interpretation and meaning, I will highly value the stories of personally acquired knowledge.

However, within any field where we are touching upon human emotion, such as parental feelings, what we construct and value is underpinned by opinions and passions that make relationships with knowledge much more complex than vying towards our preferred mode of insight and influence. Important decisions must be made, and the plethora of information bombarding parents/carers and practitioners makes decision-making difficult because each decision has positive or negative consequences for a child – for a family. Also, for many parents, and some professionals, making these all-important decisions, initially, at least, they are new to autism and have little embodied knowledge from their lives, or, in the case of professionals, their training, that can enable them to make sense of what at first is totally overwhelming. So, these parents and professionals make sense by connection to the very constructions and values that inform their decisions and enable them to take appropriate actions in other areas of their lives:

> We respond to its connections and not simply to the immediate occurrence… We may approach it, so to speak, from any one of the angles provided by its connections. We can bring into play, as we deem wise, any one of the habits appropriate to any one of the connected objects. Thus, we get at a new event indirectly instead of immediately – by invention, ingenuity, resourcefulness. An ideally perfect knowledge would represent such a network of interconnections that any past-experience would offer a point of advantage from which to get at the problem presented in a new experience…knowledge means that selection may be made from a much wider range of habits. (Dewey 1930, p.396)

However, seeing knowledge itself as a living entity, ever changing, metamorphosing and, it is to be hoped, expanding, we can only be enabled to make wise decisions and take appropriate actions as far as the current knowledge can guide and inform us. Maria Housden (2002) came to the same conclusion. Writing about decisions made regarding cancer treatments administered to her young daughter in the last year of her life, she concluded that we make the best decision we can with the information we have at the time, and if, in some future moment, a different path or course of action is revealed, we should not torture ourselves with 'if only' but comfort ourselves with the knowledge that we did our best with what we knew then.

However, sometimes new knowledge emerges that casts shadows over our current thinking and practice whilst change is still viable. In this circumstance, it can take great courage to step outside our entrenched ideas and practices, to let go and adapt appropriately to our new insights. More than that, it can take enormous compassion both to ourselves and others to know, like Maria Housden (2002), that we did the best we could with the information we previously had.

In writing this book, and looking back over my years in special education, I had a great need for this self-forgiving compassion. As previously outlined, for me knowledge flows in many streams. Academics of old had great faith in book-bound knowledge, and to me it seems that academics today have transposed this faith to research, journal articles, peer reviews and such like. Meanwhile scientists hold fast to objectivity, generalisation and external truths to be known and applied reliably. For them there is stability and comfort in believing that generalisable 'truths' are still out there, knowable, repeatable, measurable and predictable. However, during my life, while I experienced the flow of these traditional streams of knowledge, I also was fortunate to experience other sources of knowledge. In the main there are two streams of knowledge that informed my knowing in my work within the field of autism. These are the emotional and embodied streams of knowledge which I believe are both attributes of the one river of personal knowledge.

In England in the 1960s I was a child threatened with segregation for being 'feeble'. I was a child briefly removed from her family for fear that my absence from school was some cultural misdemeanour rather than the result of ill-health. In the care of the authority I became ill and was returned to my family with their word thankfully vindicated. However, the stream of emotional knowing that sources back to those scant weeks drove passionately and enthusiastically my commitment to inclusive education both as a professional and a voluntary activist within the disability movement for many, many years. It was also fed by knowledge that having been returned to my family they were urged to send me to a special school where all my medical needs could be catered for. However, the advice of my doctor and head teacher prevented my family from complying with this recommendation. Had they, I came to recognise, I would never have become a teacher, because the regime in those settings was then medical rather than educational. In fact, my common retort as a young teacher to those favouring special schools was that someone in 1960s Britain drew a line excluding those with chronic ill-health and a high incidence of school absence from ordinary classrooms; who wanted at that time to be the one drawing the line?

However, over the years of my classroom practice the struggle for inclusive education gained ground. What was once seen as eccentric and idealistic became 'politically correct'. These days it is as hard for those who argue for special schools as it once was for those, like me, who demanded inclusive mainstream schooling for all. Against this new tide that I once rode, I need the courage to admit that another stream of knowing has informed and influenced my thinking and practice.

This stream of knowing is called embodied knowledge. Its source is more than 30 years of dedicated, reflective experience and creativity in education, and it screams that 'melting-pot' inclusion does not meet the diverse needs of children.

The 'melting-pot' classroom is a hard place for both students and teachers. It is a place of normalisation. Regardless of a plethora of governmental initiatives, normalisation requires a 'dumbing down' reductionism. For example, in the late 1990s in England the numeracy and literacy hours took the vast sea of students and divided them, yet again, into ability groups within classes. Also, they attempted to make a profitable use of different learning needs and styles. What they did not do was develop a flexible, empathetic response and a celebration of difference. They presented an 'idiot's guide' to teaching, providing primary teachers with such banal information as to hold 'big' books so that a class of students could see them. In the step-by-step guide to teaching they showed little trust in embodied knowledge and experience, and inspired little creative or reflective thinking in primary teachers. However, creative and reflective teaching practices are necessary if teachers are to adapt their individual classrooms to the different strengths and needs of each year's students across a vast curriculum and its ever-expanding syllabi.

Meanwhile in Ireland the revised primary curriculum, launched in 1999, placed significant emphasis on active and collaborative learning and peer teaching. Visiting vertically grouped/cross-age primary classrooms in Ireland, one can only praise and admire the dogged determinism and conscientious effort made by teachers to make this work across the whole primary age range, all levels of ability and all learning styles and needs.

However, it is my contention that it does not and cannot. Even in the clothing industry a one-size-fits-all approach has been dogged by problems and failures. How and why do we expect the perfect uniqueness of every child to fit neatly and comfortably into one pedagogical conception of education and the nature of learning?

My embodied knowledge has influenced my emotional knowing; my emotional knowing has guided my embodied knowledge. Together, as the sum of my personal knowledge, they now argue for an alternative educational model. They do not argue for segregation but adaptation;

adaptation that is not of the child to the classroom, but of the classroom to the child. They do not argue for a teaching approach, but for a teaching philosophy that is not about fitting any child to any one form of teaching, but one that draws upon different educational philosophies and approaches as they suit the learning strengths and needs of individual children. This may seem like idealism, and I suspect and fear that many mainstream teachers will view it as onerous and impossible, asking in disbelief, 'How can one adult adapt one classroom to accommodate the different learning strengths and needs of so many divergent learners?'

My response is that inclusion is not simply about being together in one place at one time following the same or similar curriculum. Inclusion is about parity of respect and value. Therefore, for me, parity is not a generalisation but a unique understanding and appropriate adaptation to individual strengths and needs. Conflictingly, reductionism to 'one size fits all' ultimately disrespects and devalues all, as it espouses a common denominator that exists more in theory than practice; more in numbers than with human beings. Therefore, beyond the simple adaptations that I argue every classroom needs to accommodate the strengths and needs of students with autism and visual learners, I also voice the proposal that if we are to treat all children with parity and respect within our schools there is a clear and urgent need to have classrooms in which the dominant teaching approach is not a language-based, collaborative learning one. There are children who work and learn best on their own. There are children who explore ideas best in a visual form rather than the spoken one. There are children who actively learn and work best in structured environments within time frames and routines. Not all these extra-ordinary children have autism. So, back to my initial question: 'What if we got it wrong?'

What Is Autism? The Core Differences

In 1979 Lorna Wing and Judy Gould developed a tripartite or three-way description of autism. This describes a cluster of features that continue to provide part of the diagnostic criteria for autism. They are referred to as impairments in social development, language and communication, and thought and behaviour. They are now popularly referred to as Wing's 'Triad of Impairments in Autism'.

The impairment or extreme delay in social development particularly refers to interpersonal development and is considered to stem from impaired social cognition, that is, an awareness, perception and/or reasoning regarding social interactions that differs from what is considered 'normal'. Therefore, the significant differences seen as impairments in social cognition are also those that are most likely to be the key to understanding what are considered impairments or 'deviances' in both verbal and non-verbal language and communication.

However, the separation of impairment in language/communication and social development was critically questioned and eventually amended in the *Diagnostic and Statistical Manual of Mental Disorders, Fifth Edition* (DSM-5: American Psychiatric Association 2013), which is discussed in Chapter 2.

Finally, the impairment in thought and behaviour refers to rigidity in both, which is often accompanied by a lack of imagination. In other words, this central characteristic refers to a spectrum of bias towards fact and factual recall/accounts rather than the fictional and creative.

There are two main core differences in how people with autism think and relate to the world. (Please note that I call these differences not problems or difficulties.) Many identify social cognition as the core of the difference between those with and without autism. Social cognition is the process by which we communicate and interact with other people. Since the work of the developmental psychologist Jean Piaget (1896–1980), social cognition has been described as both the ability to understand the other's feelings and the ability to take the other's perspective. Therefore, it is said that people with autism have difficulty with the type of thinking particularly crucial for interacting with other people. An experiment carried out by Baron-Cohen, Leslie and Frith in 1985 gives one of the best examples of this difference. The authors argued that it showed the difficulty children with autism have in thinking about the thoughts of others, that is, 'putting themselves into other people's shoes'. It has come to be known as the 'Theory of Mind [ToM] Experiment'.[1]

In the ToM experiment (Baron-Cohen *et al.* 1985) a child was seated at a table on which there were two dolls and two different-shaped boxes, for example one square and the other round. The researcher named the dolls for the child, for example Anne and Mary, and then checked that the child had understood which was which. Then, doll Anne was seen to put an object into the square box while doll Mary watched. Doll Mary was then removed while doll Anne took the object out of the square box and put it into the round one. When doll Mary returned, the child was asked three questions: (1) 'Where will Mary look for her xxx?' (2) 'Where is the xxx really?' (3) 'Where was the xxx in the beginning?' Baron-Cohen *et al.* (1985) considered question one a personal belief question, the second question a reality one and the third a memory question. They tested three groups of children, as seen in Table 1.1, with their results depicted in Table 1.2.

Table 1.1 The three groups of participant children
in the 'Theory of Mind' experiment.

Group 1: 20 children with autism	Group 2: 14 children with Down's syndrome	Group 3: 27 children without special educational needs
Average chronological age: 11.11 years	Average chronological age: 10.11 years	Average chronological age: 4.5 years
Average mental-non-verbal age: 9.3 years	Average mental-non-verbal age: Lower than Group 1	
Average mental-verbal age: 5.5 years	Average mental-verbal age: Lower than Group 1	

Source: Baron-Cohen *et al.* 1985.

Table 1.2 Results of the 'Theory of Mind' experiment.

Group 1: 20 children with autism	Group 2: 14 children with Down's syndrome	Group 3: 27 children without special educational needs
Belief Question 1: 8% accuracy	Belief Question 1: 86% accuracy	Belief Question 1: 85% accuracy
Reality Question 2: 100% accuracy	Reality Question 2: 100% accuracy	Reality Question 2: 100% accuracy
Memory Question 3: 100% accuracy	Memory Question 3: 100% accuracy	Memory Question 3: 100% accuracy

Source: Baron-Cohen *et al.* 1985.

As shown in Table 1.2, the results for the belief question were significantly different for the children with autism compared to the other two groups. When asked 'Where will Mary look for her xxx?' most children in Group 1 had pointed to the present location of the object rather than where it had originally been placed. However, Baron-Cohen *et al.* (1985) concluded that, as the children with autism had scored 100 per cent accuracy in both the reality and memory questions alongside their peers without autism, this signified that their inability to 'put themselves into others' shoes' or 'egocentrism' (as it has been called) is conceptual rather than perceptual. In other words, whilst children with autism see the world as others see it, they apparently cannot appreciate what others are thinking or see the world from another's perspective. It is important to note that children without autism begin to develop the ability to take on other people's mental perspectives at a very young age. Some psychologists have suggested that this ability, known as 'conceptual role-taking', may be possible as early as two years of age.

From the 1985 experiment Baron-Cohen went on to further develop the ToM in relation to autism. By the end of the 1980s he was arguing that the significant difference noted in the 1985 experiment might explain why children with autism display 'odd' behaviours. He speculated that the difficulty children with autism experienced with thinking about the thoughts of others extended to reflecting on their own thoughts. Whilst the first is necessary for complex social behaviour (interpersonal), the second is necessary for complex individual behaviour (intrapersonal).

Since these findings, Baron-Cohen has developed the idea that a different social cognition is the core of autism rather than impairment. In his book *The Essential Difference* (2003) he proposed that underlying this difference there may be an 'empathy–systemising' (E–S) spectrum that concurs with gender differences which are perhaps evolutionarily derived to ensure the survival and propagation of the species. In other words, the female brain is more predisposed to empathy and the male brain to systemising. Baron-Cohen defines empathising as 'the drive to identify another person's emotions and thoughts and to respond to them with an appropriate emotion' (2003, p.2). He defines systemising as 'the drive to analyse, explore and construct a system'

(2003, p.3). From this viewpoint, he proposes that autism is the result of an extreme male brain which may result from a surge of excessive foetal testosterone hormone during pregnancy. He and his colleagues have undertaken longitudinal studies to investigate this theory.

Also, Baron-Cohen took the initial idea of social cognition and broke it down into two components. These are the cognitive and affective components. Whereas the cognitive aspect of empathy enables one to use ToM, or 'mind-read' as it may more commonly be called, the affective component enables the appropriate emotional response to the other's emotional state. As seen in the ToM experiment, the affective component may be absent in persons with autism because the cognitive component is missing or reduced.

However, there is a growing concern that much of the past and present research, and the acquired knowledge in the field of autism, has an 'outsider' looking-in stance. There are other sources of insight regarding autism that provide an 'insider's' view of how people with autism perceive and make sense of the world. While these alternative sources of personal knowledge do not contradict Baron-Cohen's 'male brain' theory, they do not look at the 'systemising' brain from the magnifying glass viewpoint.

Beyond these personal, insightful accounts, there is the other stark and disturbing reality of the disproportionate number of adolescents and adults with autism who suffer with depression and anxiety. Whether the affective component is absent as Baron-Cohen proposes or the cognitive component is missing or reduced as Wing's 'Triad of Impairments in Autism' theorises, it is clear from these figures that people with autism are capable of a rich but troubled emotional response to the world and/or their interactions in it. Again, this raises the question, 'What if we got it wrong?'

Note

1. The term 'Theory of Mind' (ToM) is attributed to Davin Premack and Guy Woodruff (1978). It refers to the ability to attribute mental states to oneself and others, appreciating that others may have constructions, beliefs, feelings, etc. that are different from one's own. Premack and Woodruff (1978) proposed that chimpanzees and other non-human primates had the ability to understand the intentions of others and therefore possessed ToM.

Chapter 2

AUTISM

A Recent Story

Introduction

In this chapter I relate the history of the emergence and development of our current construction of autism as I came to understand it. I include this chapter because I believe that without the knowledge of the history of autism we cannot make informed choices or draw informed conclusions, or, as Dewey (1930, p.398) succinctly wrote, 'We cannot entertain the conception of a world in which knowledge of its past would not be helpful in forecasting and giving meaning to its future.' I also include this chapter because in my time within the field of education I saw much to support Santayana's (1905) viewpoint that 'those who cannot remember the past are condemned to repeat it', albeit in slightly different forms.

Nevertheless, I appreciate that, for some, a chapter dedicated to the history of how we arrived at our current construction of autism may seem unpalatable, representing too much technical/scientific information. Therefore, whilst urging the reader to slowly wade through it, I also offer the reassurance that in constructing this book I endeavoured to write chapters so that they could be read independently of each other. That said, I sincerely believe that only awareness of the history of autism can provide the essential prerequisite necessary to understanding methods and approaches currently being developed and advocated.

Autism: The Past

For me, the story of our present-day construction of autism begins in 1943 with Leo Kanner. Kanner was a psychiatrist from Boston, USA. It is acknowledged that he coined the term 'early infantile autism' in describing the predominant features of a group of his young patients who were presenting with similar symptoms. These were:

- a profound autistic withdrawal[1]

- an obsessive desire for preservation of sameness

- a good rote memory

- an intelligent and pensive expression

- mutism, or language without real communicative intent

- over-sensitivity to stimuli

- a skilful relationship to objects.

From this work, the term autism came to describe a specific disorder with a characteristic set of symptoms rather than a definitive class of biological or genetic features. In other words, autism was diagnosed by behavioural factors that were either present or absent, that is, how the person behaved or failed to behave rather than physical, measurable qualities or quantities observed in diseases, such as polio or mumps.

Then, in 1979, following decades of debate and research, Lorna Wing and Judith Gould concluded that the difficulties associated with autism could be described as a 'Triad of Impairments':

1. impairment of social interaction

2. impairment of social communication

3. impairment of social imagination, flexible thinking and imagination.

Also, between the intertwining decades from Kanner (1943) to Wing and Gould (1979), three distinctive schools of inquiry emerged into the possible cause/s of autism. These were:

1. the emotional and environmental theory

2. the ethological theory

3. the genetic/organic theory.

In my opinion, it is important to understand the theories proposed by these three approaches because, regardless of evidence to prove or disprove any of them, their influences continue to permeate present thinking and methods. Overall, as will be seen within the following three sections, these differing schools of thought took either nurture or nature constructions of the cause/s of autism.

The Emotional and Environmental Theory

Kanner (1943), in his original description of autism, suggested that the parents of children with autism tended to be highly intelligent, obsessive people who were interested in abstractions and lacking in real human warmth. In so doing, he was situating the cause of autism within the nurture hemisphere of the argument.

Bettelheim (1967), developing Kanner's (1943) line of thought, argued that mothers of children with autism lack the capacity to develop full emotional relationships with their children. He proposed that the child interprets the mother's emotional inadequacy to mean that she finds contact with him/her unpleasant and undesirable. The child then withdraws from this distressing and disturbing contact, initiating a cycle in which the child becomes increasingly isolated from first his mother, and then other members of his/her family.

Clancy and McBride (1969), building on Bettelheim's (1967) work, studied 53 children with autism and their families within family therapy situations. They expressed the belief that their findings indicated that mothers fell into a 'type':

> We have noted that mothers are practical, capable people, tend to be the dominant marriage partner, and carry the family through difficulties calmly and efficiently. They give great attention to detail, and become upset easily in the face of seemingly trivial incidents. (Clancy and McBride 1969, p.235)

They proposed that this maternal 'type' was one of two contributory elements in the formation of abnormal patterns of interaction between the child, mother and other members of the family.

The other element postulated was the 'abnormal' behaviour the child exhibited in his/her early years. This finding was arrived at through retrospective interviews with the mothers of the children with autism involved in the study. It proposed that the children had exhibited a pattern of 'abnormal' behaviours which had included the following features:

- lazy sucking associated with long and tiresome feeding periods

- absence of the smiling response

- quiet, undemanding behaviour when left alone, but irritation when disturbed

- unresponsiveness to the human voice.

Supporting Bettelheim's (1967) proposition, they concluded that these two elements construct an 'initiating context' in which the mother–child relationship breaks down by becoming progressively negative.

From this conclusion, many studies of the personality characteristics of parents with children with autism followed. For example, McAdoo and DeMyer (1978) administered a personality test to parents of children with autism and to another group of parents with children with emotional/behavioural disorders. Their results showed few, if any, differences between the personality characteristics of the two groups of parents, from which McAdoo and DeMyer (1978) made the conclusion that this suggested that parents of children with autism are similar in personality to those of other children with psychological problems. However, consideration as to the psychological stresses and distresses on either group of parents was not made.

Furthermore, other studies of this era and within this school of thought, such as Goldfarb (1961), even suggested evidence of personality abnormalities among the parents of children with autism. Then, finally, a careful and methodical review carried out by Cantwell and Baker (1984, p.42) of all such studies concluded that the hypothesis 'the presence of deviant parent–child communication or interaction patterns' or 'the presence of parental psychiatric disorder or deviant personality characteristics' was not supported in the literature of the day.

However, the story of the theory that autism is nurtured by emotional and environmental elements had another dimension that should be noted. Clancy and McBride (1969) also suggested abnormal patterns of interaction within the families of children with autism. They proposed that it was not only the personality characteristics of the mother/primary carer or parents that contributed to the formation of abnormal patterns of interaction, but the way in which all family members communicated and interacted with each other. However, studies to confirm this proved problematic. For example, interviews with parents may have knowingly or unknowingly distorted accounts as to what went on between family members, and researchers may have been influenced by their knowledge that one family member had already been diagnosed with autism. Therefore, in the review Cantwell and Barker (1984) undertook, they concluded that the evidence that familial communication problems contributed to a predisposing factor in the development of autism was not strong.

Nevertheless, there was a point that did emerge from studies of the family environments of children with autism which may be worthy of mention. This was that their home environments may well differ from that of children with no autism because of the autism rather than as the cause of it. For example, DeMyer (1979) described some of the effects upon families with a child with autism. These included parental struggles with toileting, eating, teasing and jealousy. However, DeMyer's (1979) study of 59 siblings of children diagnosed with autism and 67 siblings of children without autism also noted the same issues in both groups. Thus, although the belief that the home environments of children with autism may differ because of autism may have become established in contemporary thought, from DeMyer's (1979) study it was not clear that the concerns noted resulted from the presence of a child with autism.

The Ethological Theory

This was the theory espoused by Nikolaas Tinbergen, an ethologist. An ethologist makes detailed observations of the different behaviours displayed by an organism, and of the frequency with which these occur over a given period. No attempt is made to influence the environment. Ethologists use their observations to argue that organisms display instinctive patterns of behaviour which serve important functions, such as obtaining food, water and sexual partners. Ethological studies of both primates and humans have proposed that from birth there is a basic motivation to communicate and form social bonds with other members of the species, particularly the immediate family. Also, older children have been seen to use a wide range of behaviours to form bonds both within and beyond their families.

Nikolaas Tinbergen proposed an ethological theory of autism. In it he argued that the lack of motivation to form social bonds was central to the predisposition of a child with autism. Furthermore, he proposed that this lack of motivation was the innate cause of autism. In other words, Tinbergen proposed that the cause of autism was within the nature of the child, not the nurturing s/he receives.

In 1983 Tinbergen and Tinbergen, who were by then a husband and wife team, made detailed studies of the behaviour of children with autism in different settings, such as homes and schools. From these studies, they argued that whilst these children possess the basic human motivation to approach other people and form social bonds, their motivation is offset by anxiety which produces an unusually powerful motivation to avoid such encounters or what they termed 'motivational conflict'. They suggested that this 'motivational conflict' may lead to three different outcomes. These are:

1. 'Avoidance' motivation: In this scenario the child is driven to behaviours that protect her/him from contacts with others, for example avoidance of eye contact and staring beyond and through others.

2. 'Approach' motivation: In this scenario the child will attempt social contact but is only able to make tentative approaches towards others, for example approaching but with head hanging and/or standing side-on.

3. The 'approach' and 'avoidance' motivation: In this scenario the child is unable to either approach or avoid. This results in

behaviour/s that show signs of extreme frustration or anxiety, for example temper tantrums, head banging and/or other repetitive actions.

Tinbergen and Tinbergen (1983) concluded that all the behaviour patterns characteristic of autism are expressions of motivational conflict which, over time, inhibit the normal development of the child. For example, the child's failure to interact socially and to communicate with speech and/or gesture occurs because the child is too anxious to engage in social contact. Then the child's repetitive activities and restricted interests develop because anxiety inhibits flexibility of behaviour.

Additionally, in 1978, before Tinbergen and Tinbergen's (1983) study, Richer, working within Tinbergen's ethological construction of autism, also suggested that the anxiety-driven tendency of a child with autism encourages 'approach' behaviours from adults who are unconsciously trying to overcome the child's avoidance. Richer (1978) concluded that this has exactly the opposite effect from what is intended because it drives the child into further avoidance behaviours. Ultimately this creates a vicious circle in which the more the adult approaches the child, the more the child withdraws, becoming increasingly isolated. To support his hypothesis Richer studied a group of children with autism and a group of children without autism, and their teachers. He classified behaviours into 'social approach' and 'social avoidance' to compare the amount of time each group of children spent on each type of behaviour and the amount of time the teacher spent on approach and avoidance behaviour towards each group of children. He found that children with autism spent significantly less time than their counterparts without autism on 'approach' behaviour, such as talking and pointing. Also, they spent significantly more time on 'avoidance' behaviour, such as turning away. However, whilst these findings are not necessarily surprising, Richer (1978) also found that teachers tended to spend more time on certain 'approach' behaviours towards children with autism than their peers without autism, for example touching and looking at them. However, this was also offset against an equal extent of many other teacher behaviour patterns with both groups, for example guiding the child's hand.

However, in a later study questioning Richer's (1978) findings, Clark and Rutter (1981) found that increasing social demands made children with autism increase the amount that they interacted with others, although the quality of these interactions remained 'unusual'. This fitted with previous findings by Hermelin and O'Connor (1970) that children with autism engage in the same amount of eye contact but it is the pattern that is unusual.

Tinbergen and Tinbergen (1983) also identified a range of traumatic events in early childhood which they argued made a child with autism abnormally anxious about the process of bonding. This list included:

- an early period of hospitalisation

- an early period of separation from the family

- a physical difficulty, such as loss of hearing or vision.

However, as many children experience these without developing autism, Tinbergen and Tinbergen's conclusions could not explain why some develop autism and others do not. Richer (1983), in a supportive response in the same year, argued that children with autism possibly possess an inherited heightened vulnerability to trauma. This suggestion of a genetic predisposition brought the ethological theory close to the third theory of a genetic and/or organic cause.

The Genetic/Organic Theory

The third school of thought was that autism had a genetic/organic cause. Therefore, as with the ethological theory, this is a viewpoint that sees autism arising from the nature and not the nurture of the child. However, this is referring to the genetic or organic nature of the child rather than the psychological or emotional nature; in other words, hereditary factors rather than dispositional or personality ones.

The genetic/organic theory was spearheaded by several studies of the incidence of autism in families with children with autism which focused upon occurrence in both members of identical twin pairs. These studies suggested that the number of cases in which both members of a twin pair develop autism is greater for identical than for non-identical twins, indicating a genetic predisposition.

An example of one such study was Folstein and Rutter's (1978) study of 21 same-sex pairs of twins between the ages of 5 and 23, each including one twin with autism. Eleven of these twin pairs were identical and ten were not. Of the eleven identical twin pairs, four both had autism, whilst in the case of the ten non-identical twin pairs, none both had autism. Also, most significantly in the same study, Folstein and Rutter (1978) found that almost all the identical twins not conforming to the diagnosis of autism showed some autistic tendencies, particularly with spoken language. These findings suggested that a substantial proportion of children with autism or exhibiting what may be described as autistic tendencies have inherited a genetic predisposition to develop in this way.

Once a genetic factor was accepted, the question arose as to what type of 'defect' might be transmitted by the gene. In the scientific world of medicine, it is common to assume that if a difference, which is viewed as a disorder, has a genetic basis, then an organic defect can be found, for example a structural or functional abnormality of part of the brain. This assumption brings us to current theories.

Autism: The Present

Our present knowledge and understanding of autism is still evolving. However, it is now generally agreed and accepted that autism is caused by neurological difference. There has been much research and many theories as to the exact nature of this neurological difference. The pervasiveness of autism has generally led researchers to look for differences on a hemispheric level. In other words, because of the overall global effect of autism across multiple cognitive functions, researchers have tended to look for differences in either the right or left-brain hemisphere rather than attempting to pinpoint precise areas of the brain. There are a few notable exceptions to this.

One of these is the amygdala theory proposed by Baron-Cohen in the 1990s. This theory was based on observed differences in the amygdala in the brain images of adults with autism. The amygdala is an almond-shaped mass located deep within the temporal lobe of the brain (Figure 2.1). It is situated in the paleomammalian brain, which consists of the septum, hypothalamus, hippocampal complex, cingulate cortex and the amygdala, and is now popularly termed the 'limbic system' (MacLean 1952).

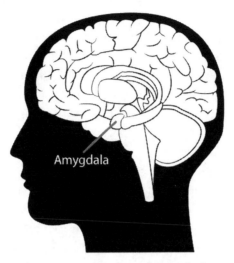

Figure 2.1 The position of the amygdala in the human brain.

MacLean (1952) was the first person to recognise the limbic system as a major functioning system in the brain. In doing so he claimed that this set of structures arose in early mammalian evolution and that it is responsible for the emotional and motivational instincts and responses involved in survival. These include feeding, reproductive and parental behaviours. In this way, the paleomammalian brain or limbic system, which is anatomically the midbrain, is considered the emotional centre of the brain.

Moreover, within this over-arching system, the amygdala is believed to be involved in the automatic processing of emotions, such as fear, anger and pleasure. Also, the amygdala is thought to be responsible for determining what and where memories are stored in the brain. This is believed to be determined by how big an emotional response an event invokes. Therefore, observed differences in the amygdala in adults with autism led Baron-Cohen to propose that people with autism have deficits in 'social intelligence' that may be caused by what he termed as an 'abnormality' (Baron-Cohen *et al.* 2000).

Alongside the amygdala theory is another notable exception to the search for differences on a hemispheric level that should be mentioned.

It is the theory of mirror neurons (MN). Again, this is research that pinpoints a specific brain region as the possible site responsible for the differences seen in the development of autism within individuals.

My introduction to this theory occurred in July 2005. Before that time I had worked in the field of special education for many years. During those years autism had held a special fascination for me. I was determined to know the cause of autism within my lifetime, and to that end I took on extra study and reading. This included a psychology degree. Then in 2005, during the final year of this degree, I felt for the first time that this goal was attainable. The reason for this was the mirror neuron theory. This is how it came about.

I was attending a summer school. It was the custom and practice at these for tutors to present evening papers in which they related their research interests. One evening I attended one of these lectures at which a tutor described a neurological phenomenon called 'mirror neurons' first discovered and reported by Di Pellegrino *et al.* (1992) from their research with primates. They described a neural basis that was not focused on the various deficits in cognitive functioning commonly attributed to people with autism. Instead, the MN theory focuses on an imitative disturbance involving difficulties both in copying actions and inhibiting more stereotyped mimicking, such as is seen in the presentation of echolalia, that is, the meaningless repetition of spoken words that often includes phrases from television programmes and/or advertisements. This neural basis is proposed to originate in the class of neurons in the frontal cortex now known as the mirror neurons. These neurons have been observed to activate in relation to both specific actions performed by an individual (self) and matching actions performed by others (other), suggesting a potential bridge between minds. Also, the theory proposes that, as these MN systems exist in primates who do not exhibit imitative and 'ToM' abilities, for them to have developed to perform social cognitive functions, sophisticated cortical neuronal systems must have evolved in humans in which this system functions as a key element. Therefore, the conclusion drawn by researchers in this area is that early disturbances and/or failures in the development of the MN system within the brain of an individual is highly likely to result in a consequent cascade of developmental impairments as characterised by autism spectrum disorders.

However, in contrast to both the amygdala (Baron-Cohen *et al.* 2000) and the MN theories, since the emergence of the neurological construct of autism it has been hypothesised that, given the pervasiveness or global nature of the condition, the difference may be at a hemispheric level. The human brain is composed of two distinct hemispheres which are connected in the middle by a bundle of nerve fibres called the corpus callosum (Figure 2.2).

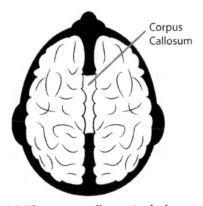

Figure 2.2 The corpus callosum in the human brain.

The corpus callosum acts as a super-fast motorway connection between both hemispheres of the brain, which when working well enables co-ordinated and integrated thought.

From the onset of the neurological construction, many scientists, professionals and persons with autism have hypothesised that the difference would be found in the right side of the brain. However, more recent brain scanning imagery of persons with autism claim to have observed volumetric and geometric differences in the left brain (Ecker 2010).

One of the most popular 'right-brain difference' theories stems from an idea proposed by Norman Geschwind and Albert Galaburda (1987) called the Geschwind–Galaburda hypothesis. This theory explains why males and females have different maturation rates between cerebral hemispheres. In the theory, male brains mature later than females, with right hemispheres maturing before the left. They proposed that this was the result of testosterone levels, with sexual maturation fixing the hemispheres at relatively different stages of development after puberty. The theory is based upon the simple observation that testosterone secretion has three developmental surges. The first surge is during the pre-natal period at around 8 to 24 weeks into the pregnancy. The second surge is approximately around the fifth month after birth. The third and final surge is the one we are all more familiar with, the surge at puberty. From this the speculation that the pre-natal surge of foetal testosterone affects the growth rate of the two hemispheres of the brain was arrived at, with the hypothesis that the more foetal testosterone released the quicker the right hemisphere will develop, and correspondingly the slower the left hemisphere develops.

In 1997 Baron-Cohen and Hammer drew upon this theory, proposing that hormones may be the cause of the sex differences in the mind. Hence, alongside the amygdala theory of autism which constructs autism as the result of a brain abnormality, since the end of the 1990s Baron-Cohen has also been influential in the promotion of a 'gender difference' model of autism. In this model he proposes that typical sex differences may provide a neurobiological and psychological understanding of autism. This constructs autism as an extreme version of the male brain. It has led Baron-Cohen (2003) to situating the ToM within the broader domain of empathy, with the introduction of a new construct which he has entitled 'systemising'. This has been called the 'empathising–systemising theory' (E–S) of autism.

In traditional medicine and cognitive psychology, the right hemisphere is attributed with spatial ability functions, and the left hemisphere with the language and communication roles. Baron-Cohen's (Baron-Cohen and Hammer 1997) 'extreme male brain theory' of autism sees autism as being on a continuum of sex difference with individual differences in the general population. The theory proposes that at a biological level the cause of autism may be 'hyper-masculinisation' resulting from higher than normal levels of foetal testosterone stimulating the growth of the right brain and inhibiting the growth of the left brain. This hypothesis also conjectures that certain features of autism, such as obsessions and repetitive behaviour, that were previously regarded as 'purposeless', are highly purposeful and intelligent, that is, 'hyper-systemising'. In his book *The Essential Difference* Baron-Cohen (2003) proposes that they are a sign of a different way of thinking. Interestingly, this theory has also led to much speculation that boys and girls require different educational approaches. However, in writing this book, one of my greatest hopes is that the requirement of an alternative pedagogy based on neurological thinking rather than gender will be recognised, because whilst hyper-systemising may predominantly affect males, it certainly crosses genders.

However, in November 2010, I attended the 'Seeing the Light Conference', funded by Research Autism, which was to overturn everything I had previously thought regarding which hemisphere played the influencing role in the development of autism. In some ways, it challenged the medical and more traditional, psychological right-brain theories whilst ironically reinforcing more popular constructions of the functions of the left- and right-brain hemispheres.

I will return to this conference and the epiphany I experienced in the next chapter. For now, the important aspect to note is that in her conference paper Dr Christine Ecker from the Department of Forensic and Neurodevelopmental Sciences at the Institute of Psychiatry in King's College, London, stated finding no significant difference in right-brain scans but significant difference in left-brain scans between adults with and without autism. They divided these observed differences into the two sub-groups of volumetric and geometric features. The volumetric features are cortical thickness and surface area. The geometric features are the cortical folding, depth and curvature.

Previously I noted that traditional medicine and cognitive psychology attribute the right hemisphere as being involved in spatial ability and the left hemisphere in language and communication. Much of these conclusions are based on hard evidence emerging from well-documented brain injuries, experiments, scans and so forth. One well-known example of such documented evidence was the work of Pierre Paul Broca who reported the loss of the ability to speak in two patients following injuries to their posterior inferior frontal gyrus (Figure 2.3). Broca is credited with the identification of Broca's area, a region in the frontal lobe of the dominant hemisphere of the human brain (Figure 2.4). The dominant hemisphere is usually the left one, and Broca's area has been seen to have functions linked to the production of speech. Since his discovery, the loss of the ability to speak following such injury has become known as Broca's aphasia or 'expressive aphasia'.

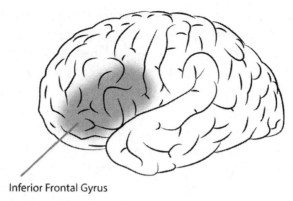

Inferior Frontal Gyrus

Figure 2.3 The inferior frontal gyrus in the human brain.

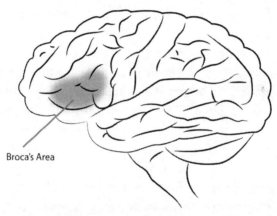

Broca's Area

Figure 2.4 Broca's area within the inferior frontal gyrus in the human brain.

However, alternative views of the functions of the two hemispheres have emerged in the public domain via the influence and prestige of persons, such as neurophysiologists, and contemporary developments in neurodevelopmental interventions, such as Brain Gym. Generally popular psychology describes the left brain as the logic hemisphere and the right brain as the gestalt hemisphere. I use the word 'generally' because this theory also allows for the reversal in some rare individuals. The logic or left hemisphere is held to process information from pieces or details to the whole in a linear or sequential, structure-orientated manner, while the gestalt or right hemisphere is believed to process information from the whole down to the integral pieces in a contextual or situational, people-orientated manner. Therefore, where traditional medicine and cognitive psychology assigns responsibility for language and communication to the left hemisphere of the brain, popular psychology, whilst taking on the construction of the left brain as the language hemisphere, holds that it processes only pieces of language, for example the alphabet, words, syntax and spelling. It is the right or gestalt hemisphere that provides the function of putting together the parts that enable language comprehension. For example, the right brain is thought responsible for putting together a string of individual words to form meaning conveyed in whole sentences or phrases. Also, it is popularly held that this meaningful comprehension involves a process that includes imagery, rhythm, movement, emotion and intuition. In other words, in relation to language, the right hemisphere provides the images, emotions and dialect that enable appropriate use and understanding.

From this we can see that there is the description of a process in which the left or logic hemisphere receives the components of language and the right or gestalt hemisphere provides the imagery and emotional context. Between the two hemispheres, as noted earlier, the corpus callosum, acting as a bridge, allows access to both the linear details of the left, logic brain and the overall meaning, emotion and imagery of the right, gestalt brain.

Interestingly, more recently, traditional science has shifted slightly towards this alternative viewpoint of where language is processed in the brain. Research evidence has emerged that metaphor is processed in the right hemisphere. Metaphor is a figure of speech in which a word or a phrase that is outside literal application to an object or action is used to describe or elaborate on it, for example 'a sea of grief' and 'heartbreak'. Moreover, metaphor is an area of noted difficulty for persons with autism who tend towards more literal representations of fact.

Where do these theories and their conflicting ideas leave those living with autism or hands-on workers in the field? Despite controversy as to what the exact nature of the neurological difference is, there is a growing clarity that we are dealing with 'difference', not 'impairment'. Indeed, it has become increasingly popular to identify this 'difference' with idiosyncratic giftedness and/or eccentric genius, especially on the part of the spectrum reserved for those with what was termed Asperger's syndrome (AS).[2] This may be a backlash to the years of misunderstanding and misguided so-called 'cures', and as such it is perfectly understandable. However, it does serve to separate out a small minority of persons with autism from their peers whilst leaving the majority with no compensation. Therefore, I propose that the current way forward is a total recognition that the whole group of persons with autism think differently rather than a very specific elevation of the possible giftedness of a minority sub-group.

The DSM-5

No reference to the present state of autism awareness would be fit for purpose without a brief description and analysis of the *Diagnostic and Statistical Manual of Mental Disorders, Fifth Edition* (DSM-5) (American Psychiatric Association 2013). This manual guides the diagnosis of autism in many countries, including the USA and Ireland. However, it is an American publication, and most diagnoses in the United Kingdom are based on the International Classification of Diseases (ICD), which is published by the World Health Organization (WHO). Nevertheless, despite having two sources of identification and diagnosis, the previous DSM-IV and the current ICD-10 were practically identical, with rare exceptions such as diagnostic names. Also, there is little doubt that the next ICD-11 will be closely aligned with the DSM-5, especially as the WHO have issued a statement promising this. The ICD-11 was to be published in 2015 but publication was deferred.

Significantly, however, it is the rare exception of differing diagnostic names that may bring less controversy for the revision of the ICD whenever it is published than the revised DSM-5 received. The DSM-5 made several changes as to how autism will henceforth be diagnosed. One of the most controversial is the removal of AS as a separate and distinctive 'disorder'. Instead AS has been incorporated as mild autism under the umbrella term of autistic spectrum disorder (ASD).

The DSM first included autism as a separate category of psychiatric 'disorder' in the DSM-III (1980) in which it was called 'infantile autism'. This was revised in 1987 to 'autistic disorder', and in 1994

Asperger's disorder (popularly known as Asperger's syndrome) was included in the DSM-IV as a separate category for the first time.[3]

However, diagnostic criteria are periodically reviewed to include new ideas, innovations and research. Therefore, the following changes made in the DSM-5 to the diagnosis of autism are part of a systematic upgrading to the entire DSM. These changes are:

- The previous terms of 'autistic disorder', 'Asperger's disorder', 'childhood disintegrative disorder' and 'pervasive developmental disorder not otherwise specified' (PDD-NOS) have been combined into one diagnosis of ASD.

- The former description of a 'triad of impairment' has been reduced to two prongs, with socialisation and communication being combined and observable across different settings and situations. The second prong remains the same, that is, repetitive behaviours and interests as outlined in Wing and Gould's 'Triad of Impairments' (1979).

- Under 'restricted, repetitive patterns of behaviour, interests, or activities', sensory behaviours are included in the criteria for the first time. These include hyper- and hypo-sensitivity and reaction to sensory input, and extraordinary interest in the sensory features of the environment.

- The emphasis during the diagnostic process has changed from giving a name to the condition to identifying all the needs a person has and how these will affect their life with the introduction of three levels of support. These are levels of severity that help to identify how much support and in what areas of function an individual has needs. Therefore, each level addresses an increasing level of need and support. A person diagnosed at level 1 requires supports that would prevent their social and communicative difficulties from being apparent. At level 2, even with supports these difficulties will still be noticeable, and at level 3, with severe social and communicative difficulties, the supports required are intensified. It is a model that reflects the existing categories of general learning disabilities, that is, mild, moderate and severe/profound.

Besides these changes to the identification and diagnosis of ASD, a new 'disorder' has been added to the DSM-5. This is called 'social (pragmatic) communication disorder' (SCD). This new 'disorder' has brought with it further controversy because some children who previously would have been diagnosed with ASD will now receive this new diagnosis. Indeed, early 'field trials' of the SCD definition, prior to the DSM-5 release, involving those already diagnosed with autism, predicted approximately a 10 per cent shift in ASD diagnosis to SCD. This prediction was amplified by a study carried out by Kim *et al.* (2014) with over 55,000 Korean children, which concluded that approximately 22 per cent of the children who had previously been diagnosed with PDD-NOS and 6 per cent of those previously diagnosed with AS would probably now receive a diagnosis of SCD. Therefore, for all concerned, an understanding of what is meant by SCD has become a priority.

Pragmatics concerns itself with the reasons why we use language to interact and the way in which we do. Therefore, pragmatics can be seen to be the area of language and communication that looks at situational speech or, perhaps more aptly, social communication. Social communication implies adaptations that take into consideration people, places and contexts. For example, children usually talk more casually and freely with their friends than with teachers and other professionals. Also, within the school context they generally speak more quietly in the classroom than in the playground. However, children diagnosed with SCD, as with many children with autism, may not be able to make these differentiations because they may not verbally and non-verbally appreciate social contexts. They may also have difficulty using communication appropriately and struggle to understand conversational rules, such as turn taking. This may lead them to talk in inappropriate ways with adults and leave them unable to maintain, initiate or terminate conversations. They may even experience difficulties making sense of what a speaker is saying and labour to formulate appropriate responses or utterances. Reading speech cues and deciphering meanings conveyed by underlining inflexions and tones may also prove highly challenging. For example, they may not be able to differentiate between genuine and sarcastic remarks.

Combined, these difficulties can make ordinary conversation onerous, and new situations stressful for the child with SCD.

Given the striking similarities in the challenges faced by children with SCD and those with autism, it is important to be aware of what differentiates the two diagnoses. What differentiates the two is that children with autism must present with both the two prongs of the ASD diagnosis. In other words, to be given the diagnosis of autism a child must have social and communicative needs and present with repetitive behaviours and preoccupations. Hence, children with social communication needs but without repetitive behaviours and/or restricted interests will be diagnosed with SCD, while those with both communication needs and repetitive behaviours and/or restricted interests will be diagnosed with ASD. Nevertheless, whilst the diagnosis of SCD is new and differs from the diagnosis of ASD, there is clearly reason for believing that children diagnosed with the former will benefit from educational approaches and therapies developed primarily for the latter. Indeed, I believe that the methods and approaches suggested in this book will assist both groups to learn in environments that in accommodating both their needs and strengths become less stressful and more learner friendly.

Also, as an afterthought, it is not unimaginable that, as with AS and its brief 19 years of life in the DSM manuals (1994–2013), SCD may at some future date be reincorporated under the umbrella of ASD!

Autism: The Future

As stated in the previous section, in the DSM-5 (2013) the triad has been reduced to a two-pronged diagnosis by combining social interaction and social communication as one prong and leaving rigidity of thinking/imagination as the other. In other words, Wing and Gould's 'Triad of Impairments' has been reduced to the following:

- impairment of social interaction and communication

and

- impairment of social imagination, flexible thinking and imagination.

One of the primary reasons for writing this book is a belief I hold, born of experience, that the second prong, rigidity of thinking, is not only undervalued in autism-specific interventions, but also offers insight into the long-term effects upon an individual and the nature of the pedagogy appropriate to children with autism and their visual learner peers. Also, contained within this argument is my vision of how the appropriate tailoring of education for children with autism could and would transform what is now viewed as an 'impairment' into a strength. To this end, Part II of this book provides practical guidance that again comes from embodied knowledge, and which points the way towards a future pedagogy built on what are the strengths of a mind with autism.

Notes

1. The word 'autistic' was derived from the Greek word *autos* meaning 'self'. Therefore, the term 'profound autistic withdrawal' signifies a withdrawal and isolation from the world and social contact with it.
2. Asperger's syndrome has been reclassified as 'mild autism' in the DSM-5 (American Psychiatric Association 2013).
3. It is possibly the construction and entry of AS in the DSM-IV and the European 'International Statistical Classification of Diseases' as a separate category that led to the emergence of the term 'high functioning autism'. It is equally important to note that while most people understood this term to be another name for AS, I have encountered two interpretations of its meaning: (1) What may be considered the transition from AS to autism. In other words, where people with AS were generally found to use and understand language, on a spectrum stretching from AS to severe autism, there would be transitional zones with language use and understanding gradually decreasing. In the transitional zone between AS and mild autism were the people with 'high functioning autism'. (2) What may be simply considered people with autism and higher cognitive abilities than their peers with autism.

Chapter 3

AUTISM APPROACHES
Origins and Insights

Introduction

In this chapter I look at the genre backgrounds of some of the most well-known intervention approaches used with children with autism. I do so because there is a simple, direct and causal link between autism theories and these interventions. In my practice, this meant that to fully understand and judge the purpose and aims of any suggested autism intervention approach I had to be aware of the thinking behind the method. Therefore, in this chapter I consider the different historical theories and the autism intervention approaches they, in my opinion, espoused. In doing so I attempt to show where more recent methods may have been seeded.

Approaches Stemming from the Emotional and Environmental Theorists

Not surprisingly those who hold an emotional and environmental explanation for autism favour therapeutic 'cures'. Put simply, these approaches carry the implicit message that if the roots of autism are emotional and environmental then 'curing' autism is possible through the correct emotional and environmental changes.

Bettelheim (1967), as referred to in Chapter 2, was committed to the hypothesis that autism is emotional and environmental in origin. His theory was built on the proposal that the mothers of children with autism have extremely abnormal personalities that prevent them from providing their children with the warmth and affection necessary for normal emotional development. To evidence and support this theory he designed a therapeutic approach that required children with autism to be separated from their parents and placed in a special residential centre. In his book *The Empty Fortress: Infantile Autism and the Birth of the Self* (1967) he provides both the proof of his theory and the evidence of the success of his therapeutic intervention, describing dramatic improvements in emotional adjustment, speech and behaviour of children placed in his special unit.

Over succeeding years there has been much criticism of Bettelheim's work. Particularly, critics noted that most of the children he described had reportedly developed 'normally' up to the age of four. It was only after this age that reports of regression and social withdrawal were noted. However, with autism the age of onset is earlier, under three years of age. Therefore critics concluded that Bettelheim's therapy succeeded because it was used with a group of children with emotional and behavioural needs rather than autism.

Meanwhile Clancy and McBride (1969), while working within the same construct of autism as emotional and environmental in origin, offered an alternative to the strict removal of the child from the home. Arguing that autism is the product of an abnormal pattern of interaction between a mother and her child, they designed a 'family therapy' to reverse and treat this abnormality.

Currently there are some therapy approaches that may be seen to have stemmed from the theory of autism as emotional and environmental in origin. These include therapies that take a play approach in which desired changes in the communication and behaviour of the child with autism are targeted through intensive, child-centred, one-to-one sessions. In my opinion these approaches include the well-known interventions of the Son-Rise Programme (SRP), Intensive Interaction and Floortime.

The Son-Rise Program (SRP)

Son-Rise was developed by Barry and Samahria Kaufman for their son who presented with autism. Contrary to the prevalent medical and professional opinion that autism is not a 'curable' condition, the Kaufmans claim that their son fully recovered from autism through complete submersion in their programme. The programme is a parent-directed, relationship-centred form of intensive and extensive play therapy. For this, parents are trained at the Kaufmans' Option Institute in Sheffield, Massachusetts. The training focuses upon parental attitudes regarding bonding and relationship building within a low-stimulus, distraction-free playroom equipped to ensure the child's sense of security and control over stimulation. Initially both parents and facilitators join in the child's behaviours through reflective techniques mirroring the child. Then when the child shows cues for willing engagement, the adult, in a non-coercive but highly energetic, excited and enthusiastic way, encourages more complex social activities around the child's motivators, that is, toys/activities of strong interest to the child. However, if the child moves away from the adult-prompted activity, instead of following the child's lead, the parent or facilitator engages in parallel play to maintain and further the child's trust.

The fundamental premise of this approach is that unconditional acceptance of the child and the encouragement of eye contact will enable the child with autism to choose to learn the necessary skills needed to teach him/herself to interact appropriately with others. However, such a premise is clearly underpinned by constructions stemming from the theory of autism as emotional and environmental in origin. For example:

- Parents are taught on the training programme how to unconditionally accept and interact with their child. This may be seen to imply that their child is manifesting autism because of a hostile environment in which s/he was not unconditionally accepted and was incorrectly interacted with. Simply by teaching the primary carers to effectively interact and accept the child, the child can be freed from his/her condition.

- The child is placed within a low-stimulus, distraction-free playroom equipped to ensure the child's sense of security and control over stimulation. This may be seen to imply that the child is suffering from an emotional imbalance in which the effects of insecurities and over-stimulations have resulted in an autistic withdrawal. Simply by rectifying these emotional irregularities the child can be 'cured'.

If considering the SRP, parents/primary carers and other interested persons should also be aware that the next step following the training programme is the creation of a low-stimulus, distraction-free playroom equipped to ensure the child's sense of security and control over stimulation within the child's own home environment. To do so parents have adapted rooms, garages and other available premises. They have also recruited volunteers or employed people to enable the lengthy periods of time a child usually spends in the playroom. For example, Davis (2006), in a case study she had undertaken, reported that the parents concerned spent approximately four to six hours a week in the playroom, whilst the student-volunteer-manned 'intervention team' spent about 40 to 50 hours per week.

The Kaufmans and supporters of the SRP report that provisions such as these result in improvements in social development. For example, in Davis's (2006) study she also noted key areas of improved social development. These were increased communication, eye contact and social engagement.

However, alongside these advantages there have been reported disadvantages. These include the high costs in terms of time, energy and financial commitments that start to be incurred from the moment a family embarks upon the programme. They also include the possibility that normal family life will be swallowed up by the programme's directed activities and concerns. For example, in the case of a family with more than one child, the child with autism may have playroom-bound routines and schedules that increase any separation that may already exist between him/her and his/her siblings. Indeed, in an investigative study carried out by Williams and Wishart (2003) into the experiences of families undertaking the SRP, the conclusions were that those supporting families using home-based interventions should consider the needs of the whole family, and that families embarking on such intensive interventions should consider ways in which to minimise disruptions to family life. Also, while Davis noted key areas of improved social development, she also observed 'only mild improvement' in 'ritualistic behaviors' (2006, p.3).

Furthermore, beyond the disadvantages mentioned, there is also the consideration that given the home-basis and individualised nature, with the child setting the pace and primary carers organising the programme, it has proven impossible to undertake an independent study of its efficacy to date.

Intensive Interaction

Intensive Interaction is an approach to teaching the foundations of pre-speech communication to children and adults with severe learning difficulties and/or autism. It was developed in the 1980s by a group of teachers working at the Harperbury Hospital School in Hertfordshire, UK. It was specially designed for the younger adults living in Harperbury, which was then a long-stay hospital. These younger adults had severe learning difficulties that limited their communication skills to a pre-verbal level, experienced extreme difficulties learning new skills and relating to others, and often presented with challenging, ritualistic behaviours and/or multiple difficulties.

In the 1980s behaviourism was flourishing and many of the techniques and approaches used at Harperbury were very structured, targeted and behaviourist in nature. Ultimately, this led to an inflexible curriculum which did not readily admit room for the individual interests and strengths of the students, and left the teaching staff stressed and frustrated. This in turn led to a high staff turnover and an increase in the number of young, inexperienced teachers employed. However, this growing pool of probationary teachers interested in discovering how to teach early communication were inspired by Gary Ephraim's (1979) 'mothering' argument that people with severe communication difficulties needed a holistic approach that mirrors how mothers interact with their very young babies. From this inspiration, they began to examine the existing literature on caregiver–infant interaction and, eventually, from analysis of videoed interactions between mothers and infants, they concluded that interactive play has a crucial role in the development of early communication. Therefore, they decided to incorporate interactive play into their daily routines with their young students. For example, dressing and eating activities became opportunities to prompt and reinforce skills through games, such as 'peek-a-boo'.

From these first steps the approach called 'Intensive Interaction' developed. Intensive Interaction uses the wide range of interactive

games that the teachers at Harperbury observed in the caregiver–
infant videos and saw as forming part of the earliest interactions. Also,
it assigns the teacher/caregiver the role of attracting and sustaining
the attention of the learner through pleasurable engagement. In doing
so, each interaction is usually seen as task-free.

Nevertheless, Intensive Interaction intrinsically contains the aim to
develop the communicative motivation and skills of the learner through
early, primary carer–infant interactions. Therefore, this approach
is clearly underpinned by premises that first view communicative
differences as having an emotional and environmental nature, if not
origin, and second, that they can be improved through individualised,
intensive, playful interactions. In other words, daily learning will be
furthered by pleasurable visitation of targeted communicative skills.

However, for those considering Intensive Interaction or those
already using this approach, I would like to state that in identifying
these underlying premises I am not in any way denying the usefulness
of Intensive Interaction as a positive intervention for children
with autism. On the contrary, I believe that as a regular practice with
individual children with autism it has much to recommend it. It can
be fun for both the adult–caregiver and the child, and as such an
enjoyable means of developing and promoting positive relationships
between them. Furthermore, advocates of Intensive Interactions, such
as Melanie Nind and Dave Hewett (1998 [1994]), claim that this
has a wider effect upon the young person's relationships generally
because her/his ability to communicate, and understanding of others,
develops, improving her/his quality of life:

> Intensive Interaction affects the quality of the interaction between
> the person with learning difficulties and other people with whom
> s/he comes into contact. Relationships with staff or carers, ability to
> communicate, and understanding of others will all be affected. With
> this the person's quality of life will also be affected. It is likely that the
> person will actually enjoy life more and engage in new experiences
> more readily. (Nind and Hewett 1998 [1994], p.11)

Nevertheless, as a practitioner in the field of autism for many years,
I became increasingly concerned about the many claims of different
intervention methods/approaches. One of my main concerns was

how these claims were interpreted and understood by carers and other professionals, because with children there are always emotional dimensions which should not be overlooked or ignored by advocates of any approach. Regarding Intensive Interaction, claims that the quality of interactions between the young person and other people with whom s/he comes into contact improves create a huge expectation that I would personally and professionally not wish to disappoint. Therefore, while as a practitioner who used Intensive Interaction and did indeed observe a positive impact upon my relationships with the children participants, I recommend caution. I enjoyed my sessions. In many ways, they were my preferred times with my students. Also, they nurtured my understanding and bond with individual children, and it was evident that every child I interacted with in this way enjoyed their sessions. For example, students frequently took me by the hand and led me to the playroom without prompting and/or coaxing. However, beyond the enrichment of our one-to-one relationship, I could not irrefutably state that my Intensive Interaction sessions with students positively affected the quality of relationships with others because Intensive Interaction was one amongst other methods/approaches I employed.

Floortime

Floortime is an approach contained within the Developmental, Individual-difference, Relationship-based model (DIR) developed in the late 1970s by Dr Stanley Greenspan. Greenspan (1979) contends that the DIR is a developmental model for assessing, understanding and 'treating' the strengths and weaknesses of any child and, despite the finding of the National Autism Center (NAC) that 'there is little or no evidence' for DIR/Floortime 'in the scientific literature that allows us to draw firm conclusions about *its* effectiveness with individuals with ASD' (NAC 2015, p.72), many professionals advocate it, having undergone formal training in its techniques.

Assumptions underpinning the DIR/Floortime approach include the construction of communication and social behavioural differences as developmentally delayed. Hence the model focuses on what are considered the essential steps of 'normal' neurotypical development, intrinsically implying that these have been missed by the child with autism in his/her development to date. Moreover, within the model, Floortime targets the creation of emotionally charged and meaningful learning exchanges that are believed will encourage the missed developmental steps to be learnt. Clearly, the contention that the socialisation, communication and thinking of a child can be changed through a therapy which directly works upon emotional engagement with others demonstrates an emotional and environmental interpretation of autism.

As its name suggests, Floortime is an approach that encourages caregivers to engage children at the child's level of play, which is usually on the floor. This floor play is child centred, using the preferred activities of the child to enable engagement. In other words, the adult enters the child's play/games to motivate the child to connect with him/her through the excitement of shared interests. Once engagement is achieved, the intention expands to include problem-solving challenges that inspire creative, curious and spontaneous responses. The underlying premise is that this will further the development of cognitive and emotional skills and abilities. Thus, all sessions are underpinned by the following three simple principles:

1. Enter the child's world and follow her/his lead.

2. Create challenges that encourage curiosity, creativity and spontaneity.

3. Expand interactions to embrace sensory and motor skills as well as a broad array of emotions.

Ultimately the aim of sessions is to encourage the two-way nature of neurotypical interactions in which shared attention, engagement and problem-solving feature. Therefore, whilst the adult enters the child's play/games, s/he also remains aware of the aims to (1) sustain focus, (2) increase interaction and (3) further abstract, logical thinking, and attempts to extend the play/game accordingly. For example, if a child lines up several figures, the adult might initially add to the line but then make an opposing line or add some vocalisations/verbalisations to the game. Hence, once the child is engaged, the caregiver focuses on increasing the complexity of the interaction. In this way, favourite toys may be placed in sight but out of the child's reach, necessitating the need for adult assistance to find an appropriate solution. This process is called 'opening and closing circles of communication' and it is the staple idea of the Floortime approach.

Within the 'opening and closing circles of communication', Greenspan and his colleagues (Greenspan and Salmon 1995; Greenspan and Wieder 1997) identified six developmental milestones that they argue are essential to the cognitive and emotional development of a child. These are:

1. the ability to self-regulate and have an interest in the world

2. intimacy and/or engagement in human relationships

3. the ability to undertake and sustain two-way communication with others

4. the ability to participate in complex communication

5. the ability to have emotional thought

6. the ability to have emotional ideas.

Moreover, Floortime does not target skills in isolation, but by targeting the emotional development of the child it holds that communication, motor and/or cognitive skills will develop. In other words, the premise of DIR/Floortime is that the doorway to development is emotional and relational in nature. Also, the assertion is that as children mature play/game strategies will be matched to their emerging interests and higher levels of interaction. For example, with the previous example of the adult matching a line of figures with a parallel line, counting in ones and twos could be introduced if the child had an interest in number and number operations.

For those considering Floortime, it is meant to be practised in a calm, distraction-free environment either in the child's home or in a professional playroom-type setting. Sessions provided by practitioners of Floortime can be between two and five hours in length, per day. These formal sessions include both interactions with a child and training for caregivers, because the aim for the Floortime therapist is that the principles of Floortime will become ingrained into the child's daily family life. For example, a study conducted by Greenspan and Wieder (2003) reported that the father of a child with autism had engaged in six daily Floortime sessions over three years. Although they concluded that Floortime was beneficial to the child, the impact on family life in terms of frequent, regular, long-term commitments of time and energy clearly needs to be considered.

Final Thoughts on Approaches Stemming from the Emotional and Environmental Theorists

Despite declarations of 'uniqueness' by certain approaches/therapies, it is evident from the three examples given that they are underpinned by a construction of autism as being emotional and environmental in nature, and that they share common principles and strategies. I have long seen these commonalities as having a shared historical grounding in cultural thinking and genres.

Regarding cultural thinking, all three approaches/therapies outlined arose in the 1970s and/or 1980s when child development ideas had been influenced by the emergence of inside-out constructivist concepts and humanistic psychology. The constructivist or interactionist developmental model considers people to be active agents in their own development, influenced by and influencing the external world. Meanwhile humanistic psychology emerged in the 1950s, taking an eclectic approach that was held together by three core assumptions: (1) subjective experience is central, (2) people are capable of personal agency and growth and (3) people as whole individuals need holistic approaches. Therefore, under the combined influences of these two approaches the child was no longer a miniature adult but a singularity with his/her individual developmental potential which, if nurtured and stimulated appropriately, could grow into her/his own agency. In this way, each individual child was invested with the potential to carve out his/her own future, and external factors such as economic background and class were considered the real barriers to achievement and mobility. Thus, the onus was placed on improving and/or changing external factors to liberate the potential of all children.

Simultaneously, there was a backlash against the rigid, structured approaches of behaviourism which in many ways was viewed as working from the outside-in with the premise that the child was an 'empty vessel' to be filled or moulded accordingly. Against this bipolar backdrop, approaches/therapies were rapidly emerging that clearly belonged to one or another genre. One such genre that can be seen historically to have emerged from the camp of humanistic, constructivist psychology was 'play therapy'. It is into this genre that all three approaches explored fit. For example, they all share the common staple that requires the caregiver or therapist to enter the child's world and initially follow the lead of the child. Clearly, they all 'tweak' their approach/therapy programmes with different priorities and terms but, essentially, in my opinion, they spring from the one well. Furthermore, the three examples given are not exclusive. There are other approaches/therapies that in whole or part have features of the 'play therapy' genre and share the emotional and environmental mantle. These have included 'Children's Hours', later known as 'Special Times', developed by Rachel Pinney in the 1960s and 1970s. 'Children's Hours' was an intensive, child-led play therapy that adapted and applied a method Pinney called 'Creative Listening' to her work with children. Pinney had developed the 'Creative Listening' method to encourage and further greater understanding between political opponents. Adapted and applied to her work with children, the fundamental idea was that children need regular periods of total attention from a caring adult (Pinney 1994):

> The adult supports and follows what the child is doing rather than making suggestions or giving ideas of their own. The adult uses neither praise nor blame.
>
> ... All children, whatever their circumstances, benefit from having a time and space in which to play out their thoughts and feelings with an attentive adult who receives all that is said and done without passing judgement. (Pinney 1994, p.2)

I trained in 'Special Times' over several years, but in the late 1990s it was swallowed up into 'play therapy' per se.

Approaches Stemming from Emotional and Environmental to Physiological and Environmental Theorists

Other approaches that may be seen to have stemmed from the theory of autism as emotional and environmental in origin could loosely include those that advocate 'toxic body' and/or an 'over-burdened immune system' as the root cause of autism. Clearly the focus of these theories has shifted from emotional and environmental to physiological and environmental factors indicating a different branch of the conceptualisation. Nevertheless, they remain at their core a construction of autism as an illness or a disease, and whereas the emotional/environmental branch sees therapy as the means of extinguishing autism, the physiological/environmental branch posits eradication through therapy and diet.

Overwhelmingly, for parents desperate for a 'cure', there is a plethora of these theories and their therapies and diets. However, before some of the most well known are outlined, it is also important to note the connecting threads that pervade most of these theories. These are what may be considered the over-arching theories that childhood vaccinations and 'leaky guts' play a significant part in either the cause or aggravation of autism in children. Therefore, both the vaccination contention and the 'leaky gut' debates are discussed next.

Vaccine Causes

Many studies have examined possible links between vaccinations and autism. Research has predominantly focused on the measles–mumps–rubella (MMR) vaccine because of a persistent suspicion ignited by a paper published in the *Lancet* in 1998 by Dr Andrew Wakefield and 12 colleagues that claimed it was the root cause of autism and bowel disease (Wakefield *et al.* 1998, article now retracted). Prior to this article, Wakefield had in the early 1990s published reports and a paper in the *Lancet* in which he proposed a link between the measles vaccine and Crohn's disease. However, follow-up peer-reviewed studies failed to confirm this hypothesis. Then through a meeting with Rosemary Kessick, a parent of a child with both autism and bowel problems who ran a group called Allergy Induced Autism, Wakefield turned his attention to researching a possible link between the MMR vaccine and autism.

Ultimately, this second focus of Wakefield's research was also to be discredited when the UK's General Medical Council (GMC) in January 2010 found three dozen charges proven against him. These included charges of dishonesty and the abuse of developmentally challenged children by subjecting them to unnecessary invasive medical procedures, such as colonoscopies and lumbar punctures. Following the findings of the tribunal, Wakefield was struck off the UK medical register and the *Lancet* retracted the publication.

However, despite the retraction of Wakefield's paper and the discrediting of the claim due to evidence of fraudulent research practices, the controversy raged on. In some countries, this led to a decline in vaccination rates that unfortunately resulted in the re-emergence of outbreaks of measles and mumps. This in turn caused the WHO to go on the offensive in 2010, undertaking to eradicate measles by 2015, and by 2016 they declared that measles had successfully been eradicated in 33 countries including Croatia, Denmark, Greece, Iceland, Lithuania, Montenegro, Spain, the UK, the USA and Uzbekistan. Clearly the indication is that the MMR controversy is being subjugated.

Nevertheless, the controversy has not completely disappeared. On the MMR vaccinations pose no risk side are mounting studies of support. One such American study, 'Autism occurrence by MMR vaccine status among US children with older siblings with and without autism' (Jain *et al.* 2015), hit the headlines in April 2015 after its publication in the *Journal of the American Medical Association* (JAMA). This was a large study of approximately 95,000 children with older siblings with ASD. In it the authors found that the 'receipt of the MMR vaccine was not associated with increased risk of ASD' whether children had just the initial shot under the age of two and/or the booster as well around the age of five, that is, 'no harmful association between MMR vaccine receipt and ASD even among children already at higher risk for ASD' because of an older sibling with ASD (Jain *et al.* 2015, p.1534).

On the MMR vaccinations pose risk of autism side of the argument are proponents who continue to stand their ground, their viewpoint being endorsed by several recent lawsuits awarding compensation to families whose children it was proven were damaged by the vaccine. One such ruling was made by a 'Vaccine Damage Payment Scheme' tribunal in the UK in 2010. The tribunal awarded the family of Robert Fletcher compensation because they found that on balance it was probably no coincidence he suffered his first epileptic seizure ten days after being vaccinated. Robert became severely physically and intellectually disabled following his seizures. Although the judgement has no direct bearing on the autism and MMR debate, it clearly ignites the controversy further.

Thus, while the issues on this debate remain swathed in controversy and emotion, the hypothesis that the MMR vaccine causes autism clearly stems from the school of thought that autism is physiological and environmental in nature, that is, autism is induced by an initial attack and the subsequent lodgement of the injected vaccine within the intestines of the child. As with the suspicion of the tribunal panel in the Robert Fletcher case, the argument for a causal relationship between the measles vaccine and autism ultimately seems to propose that the development of what is termed 'regressive autism' occurs because the child has a genetic predisposition to autism. In other words, the vaccination triggers the onset of the condition in children genetically predisposed to autism.

Bowel Disease Causes

This issue cannot be separated from the vaccine debate because there are two distinctive strands to the argument. The first is grounded in an increasing awareness that the prevalence of inflammatory bowel disease (IBD) is greater in people with autism than without, and the second is the ongoing anti-vaccine campaign theory that the IBD seen in children with autism is caused by the measles vaccine. For the pro-vaccine camp, there is no link between the two strands, but for the anti-vaccine camp there clearly is. To understand these issues it is necessary to outline both strands of the argument.

The first strand is the growing recognition that the prevalence of IBD is greater in people with autism than without, as observed by Doshi-Velez et al. (2015, p.2281): 'Across each population with different kinds of ascertainment, there was a consistent and statistically significant increased prevalence of IBD in patients with ASD than their respective controls and nationally reported rates for pediatric IBD.' This awareness has created a conundrum. The conundrum is whether it is autism that leads to bowel problems or bowel difficulties that contribute to autism. Thus, researchers are currently investigating if there are unusual biological differences in the bowels of people with autism. Some of these researchers claim to have observed unusual immune cell patterns with distinctive microscopic features or levels of microorganisms in the bowel tissue of some of their study participants (Finegold *et al.* 2002, 2010; Parracho *et al.* 2005). Also, some recent studies have suggested that there may be differences in the immune systems of people with autism and that these may be affecting the bowels. However, these immune differences and their uniqueness to autism are yet to be indisputably confirmed.

> Decades of research links immunological abnormalities to ASD. In light of the extensive crosstalk between the immune and neural systems, which includes shared signaling and developmental pathways, this line of research can yield important insights in atypical brain development. The nature of the connection between immunity and autism is the focus of ongoing research... Proper exploration of immunological features in autism presents an exciting opportunity to tease apart the biology of disorder, and may lead to therapeutic interventions. (Goines and Van der Water 2010, p.7)

However, what is clear is that autism is not the only condition associated with bowel problems. Several neurological conditions are known to affect bowel function. These include multiple sclerosis (MS), diabetes mellitus and Parkinson's disease. This occurs because the brain and the gut are closely connected through the nerve pathways of the nervous system. Therefore, as with these neurological conditions, how parts of the brain function with autism may be key to understanding its association with IBD.

Also, any bowel problems experienced by a person with autism may be exacerbated by dietary idiosyncrasies that are also prevalent with autism. These are known to include eating only one type of food or only food of a certain colour. Such restrictions result in a very limited and repetitive diet, which can lead to bowel problems.

The second strand of the bowel disease issue runs concurrently to the first and, as stated before, is believed by some to be interwoven into the first. The theory that the IBD seen in children with autism is caused by the measles vaccine is two-pronged, with supporters contending that samples of measles virus found in the gut tissue of children with autism can explain both the onset of their autism and their IBD. Hence in yet another area of the school of thought that autism is physiological and environmental in nature, the vaccine controversy rages on, fuelling speculation and, for many of us who seek to understand the condition, confusion.

To establish some clarity, it is possible to consider what is undeniably clear: that bowel problems are neither new nor unique to autism. Bowel diseases in persons with autism and other neurological conditions existed before the introduction of the MMR vaccine. Indeed, autism, albeit by different names and interpretations, existed before the introduction of the MMR vaccine. Furthermore, there are documented reports of children with autism and bowel problems who have never received the MMR vaccine. Finally, it is indisputably clear that research in this area has arisen from a construction of autism as being biological/physiological and environmental in nature.

Beyond the two over-arching theories that childhood vaccinations and 'leaky guts' play a significant part in either the cause or aggravation of autism in children, there are other theories that may be seen to have stemmed from the theory of autism as physiological and environmental in origin, holding at their core a construction of autism as an illness or a disease that can be eradicated through environmental changes, therapy and/or diet. These currently include the following.

Amalgam Causes

This controversy pre-dates and encompasses the autism cause debate. On the one hand, supporters of the use of amalgam (the traditional silver/black fillings in teeth) claim that it is a safe, effective and enduring method of filling dental cavities. On the other hand, since the 1840s, critics have asserted that the use of amalgam as a filling for dental cavities is unsafe because it may cause toxicities, such as mercury poisoning.

The amalgam debate can also be located under the umbrella of the vaccination controversy, with several academic papers, media articles and books claiming that many symptoms associated with autism mirror those seen in chronic mercury poisoning, that is, mercury is found in both amalgam and the preservative thimerosal (Thiomersal), which was used during the manufacturing process of some childhood vaccines to prevent the growth of microbes.[1] One such academic paper is a study reported by Bernard *et al.* (2000). In their abstract they present the following indictment of amalgam and mercury toxicity:

> Mercury (Hg) is a toxic metal that can exist as a pure element or in a variety of inorganic and organic forms and can cause immune, sensory, neurological, motor, and behavioral dysfunctions similar to traits defining or associated with autism. Thimerosal, a preservative frequently added to childhood vaccines, has become a major source of Hg in human infants and toddlers. According to the FDA and the American Academy of Pediatricians, fully vaccinated children now receive, within their first two years, Hg levels that exceed safety limits established by the FDA and other supervisory agencies. A thorough review of medical literature and U.S. government data indicates (i) that many and perhaps most cases of idiopathic autism, in which an extended period of developmental normalcy is followed by an emergence of symptoms, are induced by early exposure to Hg; (ii) that this type of autism represents a unique form of Hg poisoning (HgP); (iii) that excessive Hg exposure from thimerosal in vaccine injections is an etiological mechanism for causing the traits of autism; (iv) that certain genetic and non-genetic factors establish a predisposition whereby thimerosal's adverse effects occur only in some children; and (v) that vaccinal Hg in thimerosal is causing a heretofore unrecognized mercurial syndrome. (Bernard *et al.* 2000, p.i)

The authors of this paper also list an impressive number of characteristics shared by both autism and mercury poisoning. These include:

- social deficits, shyness and social withdrawal

- anxiety

- lack of eye contact

- irritability, aggression and temper tantrums

- impaired facial recognition

- failure to develop speech

- speech comprehension deficits

- sound sensitivity

- abnormal touch sensations and touch aversion.

(Bernard *et al.* 2000, pp.iii–v)

However, thimerosal has been removed from routine vaccines given to infants and very young children in many countries for some years now. For instance, Denmark removed thimerosal from routine early years' vaccines in 1992; New Zealand and Australia in 2000; in the USA, the last children's vaccines to use thimerosal as a preservative expired in 2003; and in the UK, children's vaccines containing thimerosal were removed from public issue towards the end of 2004. Hence, today thimerosal is generally not in children's vaccines in countries across the globe, including Ireland, and its absence ironically supports the WHO's finding that thimerosal in vaccines has not caused autism because 'five large-scale studies failed to find a link between thiomersal and autism, and, according to some studies, the incidence of autism has risen after discontinuation of thiomersal use in vaccines' (WHO 2008, p.425).

Moreover, the finding by the WHO is supported by many international studies, such as Fombonne *et al.* (2006) in Canada; Andrews *et al.* (2004) in the UK; and Price *et al.* (2010), Schechter and Grether (2008), Thompson *et al.* (2007) and Hviid *et al.* (2003) in the USA. Also, in 2004 the Institute of Medicine in the USA issued its eighth and final report entitled 'Immunization Safety Review: Vaccines and Autism', in which the committee concluded that the evidence available warrants rejection of a causal relationship between thimerosal-containing vaccines and autism. This report also concluded that the existing epidemiological evidence favoured rejection of a causal relationship between the MMR vaccine and autism. In other words, the evidence from studies into the incidences, distribution and control of the MMR vaccine and autism did not support a causal relationship between the two.

Nevertheless, presently some multi-dose preparations of influenza and hepatitis B vaccines still contain thimerosal products and these may be offered to children as part of broader routine childhood immunisation programmes in some countries, such as Canada. Also, amalgam fillings are still in regular usage, with amalgam-only restorations still freely available to children in Ireland. Therefore, despite the many academic and scientific rejections of the theory that amalgam–thimerosal is responsible for autism, this ongoing use continues to provoke opposing studies, such as the study already cited by Bernard *et al.* (2000, p.4), the theory of which is 'that autism represents its own form of Hg (mercury) poisoning':

> We maintain that the diverse phenotype that is autism matches the diverse phenotype that is mercurialism to a far greater degree than could reasonably be expected to occur by chance. Given the known exposure to mercury via vaccination of autistic children and the presence of mercury found in biologic samples from a number of autistic subjects, also described here, we are confident that our claim is substantiated. (Bernard *et al.* 2000, p.4)

Furthermore, the anti-amalgam campaigners claim that its use contributes to water and air pollution because mercury is released into the environment through the waste water from dental surgeries, and into the air from crematoriums and medical waste.

However, there is an anomaly in this controversy. Despite its support for amalgam restorations, the WHO in 2003 and 2008 appeared to offer support to the anti-amalgam–thimerosal products campaigners. It did so in 2003 by reiterating the findings of Skare (1995) and Health Canada (1997) that 'dental amalgam fillings are the primary source of mercury exposure for the general population' (WHO 2003, p.7). Then, in 2008, even after a decline in the usage of amalgam fillings and thimerosal products in children's vaccines, it released a paper in which it stated that 'health-care' facilities which include dental surgeries 'may' be 'responsible for as much as 5% of all mercury releases in wastewater' (WHO 2008, p.1). Thus, despite the established position that amalgam restorations are safe and effective held by such notable authorities as the World Dental Federation, the Mayo Clinic, the British Dental Health Foundation, the European Union's (EU) Scientific Committee on Emerging and Newly Identified Health Risks and, indeed, Health Canada and the WHO itself, the debate rages on.

Therefore, in conclusion, the only clarity upon which the merits of the argument can be judged may well be the insight that the hypothesis of the anti-amalgam campaigners rests upon the school of thought that autism is physiological and environmental in nature, that is, in the case of this argument the premise would seem to be that autism is induced by the assault of mercury poisoning upon the physiology of the susceptible child.

Hyper-Immunity and Other Immune System Causes

As previously stated, some recent studies have suggested that there may be differences in the immune systems of people with autism. However, these immune differences and their uniqueness to autism are yet to be confirmed.

Nevertheless, because these developments are regarded to be significant, they are worthy of consideration. They include Molloy *et al.*'s (2006) evidence that children with autism have more active immune systems. The immune system has two defence mechanisms. The first is called the *innate immune system*. It is present from birth and forms the first line of defence against any invading bacteria or virus. The second is called the *adaptive defence system*. This system develops in response to specific invading bodies and enables the body to build up its own individual immunities to diseases encountered over a lifetime. Essential to both systems are *cytokines*. Cytokines are chemicals that play a crucial, messenger role in enabling specific types of immune responses. For example, they control the strength, length and direction of the immune response to a specific invading bacterium or virus. Also, they regulate the repair of tissue following an injury. However, there are many cytokines and they all play different roles in an immune system's responses. For example, some stimulate the activation of an immune response, while others inhibit the response once repair or recovery has begun working together in a timely and co-ordinated way.

Molloy *et al.* (2006) were interested in the levels of cytokines called *helper T cells*. T cells are a type of white blood cell. Helper T cells are produced by a specific immune cell in the adaptive immune system, that is, the immune defence system that develops in response to invading bodies and enables the body to build up its own individual immunities to diseases encountered over a lifetime. The study focused on the helper T cells known as *Th1* and *Th2*. These specific helper T cells normally function in tandem, balancing one another by inhibiting each other's activity. However, in previous studies their role in the dysregulation of the immune system of individuals with autism has proved difficult to pinpoint because some studies have reported elevated levels of Th1 while others have found elevated levels of Th2. These opposed findings mirror the findings of a European study that reported that many individuals with autism suffer from both autoimmune disorders generally driven by Th1 and allergies generally driven by Th2. Nevertheless, the combination of autoimmune diseases and allergies is unusual because the two Th1 and Th2 systems are not ordinarily simultaneously overactive. Therefore, to understand this unusual occurrence, Molloy *et al.* (2006) compared individual cytokine levels in 20 children with autism and 20 children without autism before and after stimulation by an allergen and a toxin. They found that in the body's normal resting state before stimulation by an allergen and/or a toxin both the Th1 and Th2 cytokine levels in children with autism were higher than children without autism but that after stimulation there was no difference. From this they concluded that while the adaptive immune defence systems in both children with and those without autism are equally capable of generating an immune response, in its resting state children with autism produce greater levels of both Th1 and Th2 cytokines, which may make these children hypersensitive to environmental agents.

Molloy *et al.* (2006) also noted a surprising finding. Although the resting state of almost all the Th1 and Th2 cytokines measured were higher in children with autism than those without, the children with autism had relatively low levels of *IL-10 cytokine*. IL-10 cytokine belongs to a family of cytokines that regulate both the innate and adaptive immune defence systems. The IL-10 family cytokines are essential in maintaining the integrity and stability (homeostasis) of the cellular tissue (epithelial layers) covering the internal and external surfaces of the body, including the lining of vessels and cavities. They also drive innate immune responses in cellular tissue to contain damage caused by infections whilst facilitating tissue healing injuries caused by infection and/or inflammation. In doing so, IL-10 cytokine itself acts to repress pro-inflammatory responses. Thus, if both Th1 and Th2 cytokines are overactive, raised levels of IL-10 should also be present, but this was not the case.

Therefore, Molloy *et al.* (2006) had identified two anomalies in the immune defence systems of children with autism. The first was that both Th1 and Th2 could be active simultaneously, and the second was that this appears to occur without a proportional increase in the IL-10 cytokine that regulates them both. Furthermore, they proposed that this second finding may explain the first, that is, the dysfunction of IL-10 may explain the simultaneous activity of both Th1 and Th2 cytokines, and that this provides important insight into what were previously considered to be contradictory findings. In conclusion, Molloy *et al.* speculated that IL-10 cytokine dysfunction may leave children with autism unable to down-regulate their Th1 and Th2 cytokines, resulting in an unusual combination and overactivity of allergen and autoimmune responses.

As the research into hyper-immunity and other immune system-related theories continued, in 2010 Goines and Van der Water, having reviewed many of these studies, stated:

> The most exciting of these recent findings is the discovery of autoantibodies targeting brain proteins in both children with autism and their mothers. In particular, circulating maternal autoantibodies directed toward fetal brain proteins are highly specific for autism. This finding has great potential as a biomarker for disease risk and may provide an avenue for future therapeutics and prevention. Additionally, data concerning the cellular immune system in children with autism suggest there may be a defect in signaling pathways that are shared by the immune and central nervous systems. Although studies to explore this hypothesis are ongoing, there is great interest in the commonalities between the neural and immune systems and their extensive interactions. (Goines and Van der Water 2010, Abstract: Recent Findings)

Clearly, while research into autism and immunology thrives, driven by its own revelatory success, what remains beyond question is its innate construction of autism as being physiological/biological and environmental in nature.

Allergies and Food Intolerances and/or Sensitivity Causes

Food allergies and food intolerances are separate issues, and for this reason they are differentiated here.

Food allergies relate to hyper-immunity and other immune system theories and findings as discussed in the previous section. However, food intolerances are usually associated with a non-immune response. For example, lactose intolerance is the inability to digest the sugar in milk. This is caused by a deficiency in the intestinal enzyme lactase that breaks lactose down into two smaller sugars, glucose and galactose, which can be absorbed in the intestine.

Food Allergies

As with the word 'autism', the words 'allergy' and 'anaphylaxis' (an acute allergic reaction to a toxin or other foreign substance known as an antigen to which the body has become hypersensitive) are relatively modern terms coined in the twentieth century. The latter two arose when children fell violently ill after doctors administered sera using hypodermic syringes for the first time in history. In 1906 Clemens von Pirquet constructed the symptoms he observed as an 'altered reactivity', coining the term 'allergy'. Charles Richet (1913) coined the term 'anaphylaxis' when he described the condition he observed in animals used in immunisation experiments as 'against protection'. Thus, both allergies and anaphylaxis serve as defences against invading toxins or foreign bodies. Overall their purpose is to expel the toxins/foreign bodies as quickly as possible with reactions such as sneezing, vomiting and falls in blood pressure that reduce circulation.

Moreover, Richet's (1913) Nobel Prize-winning research identified the significant role played by the gut in allergic and anaphylaxis responses:

> We are so constituted that we can never receive other proteins into the blood than those that have been modified by digestive juices. Every time alien protein penetrates by effraction, the organism suffers and becomes resistant. (Richet 1913, penultimate paragraph)

Initially, following this, allergists believed that food allergies were caused by digestive failure or what has come to be termed 'leaky gut'.

The 'leaky gut' theory still underpins some popular ideas of the causes of autism.

'Leaky gut syndrome' is claimed to have symptoms that include bloating, flatulence, cramps and pain. At present, there is still no agreed medical opinion as to its existence, cause or treatment. However, proponents claim that diet, infections, parasites or medications, such as the MMR vaccine, damage the intestinal lining, leading to increased intestinal permeability or intestinal hyper-permeability that permits toxins and foreign bodies to leak through into the bloodstream initiating an immune response. Proponents claim that it is this immune response that leads to autism and other chronic diseases, such as coeliac and Crohn's diseases. For example, Lucarelli *et al.* (1995) published a study in which they attempted to 'verify' the theory that a diet free of cow's milk, wheat and other foods that had given a positive allergy skin test response in 36 participants with autism would impact positively on their behaviour. They concluded that hypothetically there is a relationship between infantile autism and food allergies.

Furthermore, the 'leaky gut' theory is grounded in the fact that the gut is an essential and integral part of both the body's immune system and the brain. Indeed, it is referred to as the 'second brain' because of the millions of neurons that connect it with the central nervous system. This close connection means that the gut reacts immediately when faced by either a toxin or a trauma. The reaction itself is triggered by the higher brain, which sends signals that lead to the secretion of agents that are necessary to the production of inflammation. This then is a purely protective defence response.

Proponents of the autism–leaky gut theory argue that a significantly high number of individuals with autism also have gastrointestinal problems. However, their argument presupposes the existence of the controversial 'leaky gut syndrome'. Also, it takes support from studies, such as De Angelis *et al.* (2013), that claim that the gut microbiota (i.e. the composite of organisms that live in the gastrointestinal tract) is abnormal in people with autism:

> The main biological significance of this work was related to the decreased level of some healthy promoting bacteria (e.g., *Bifidobacterium*) and metabolites (e.g., FAA, SCFA) in PDD-NOS and, especially, in AD children. Dietary implementation with prebiotics and probiotics could

be a useful tool to restore some microbial gaps (e.g., *Bifidobacterium*). Combining the results of this work with those from previous reports…it seemed to emerge that microbial indices (e.g., *Clostridium*) and levels of some metabolites (e.g., Glu, p-cresol) might be signatures for PDD-NOS and, especially, AD children. (De Angelis *et al.* 2013, Discussion: paragraph 6)

From such findings emerges the suggestion that restoring the correct gut microbial balance could alleviate some of the behaviours associated with autism.

Nevertheless, whether the gut microbiota is different in people with autism or not, the ultimate question is, does this difference cause autism or is it a consequence of it? Given the dietary challenges associated with autism, it is easy to infer that a limited/restrictive or idiosyncratic diet leads to microbiota differences. However, there are studies that appear to support the theory that the gut microbiota differences are in some way a cause rather than a consequence of autism. For example, Hsiao *et al.* (2013) published a study in which they claimed to have induced autism-like symptoms in mice by infecting pregnant mice with a virus-like molecule. They asserted that after birth the offspring of the infected mice showed altered gut bacteria compared with the offspring of uninfected mice. Also, they claimed that the infected offspring displayed 'certain behavioural abnormalities' that were partially reduced when they were treated with *Bacteroides Fragilis*, a health-promoting bacterium, concluding that microbiota differences are in some way a cause and not a consequence of autism.

Moreover, proponents of the 'leaky gut'/food allergy theory argue that studies such as De Angelis *et al.* (2013) and Hsiao *et al.* (2013) support their claim that the differences in gut microbiota emerge from 'leaky gut' food or vaccine allergies. As with the virus-like molecule the pregnant mice were infected with, allergic reactions to foods and/or vaccines damage the intestinal lining as well as altering the microbiota balance of the gut. Also, the damaged lining allows substances to pass into the bloodstream that then harm the higher brain. They propose that treatment with a healthy probiotic bacterium may reduce some behaviours associated with autism by increasing the robustness of the intestines and thereby limiting or preventing further leakage.

In contrast to this pursuit of a definitive, 'leaky gut', microbiota cause of autism, autism itself remains a complex condition with, I believe, a heterogeneous interplay of factors, including genetic and environmental ones. Whilst this is only my opinion, it may explain why probiotics have only partially reduced some behaviours associated with autism.

Food Intolerances

Food intolerances are commonly associated with a non-immune response. A well-known example is lactose intolerance, that is, the inability to digest the lactose in milk sugar. This condition can cause stomach pain, bloating and diarrhoea. Proponents of a role for food intolerances in the cause and/or exacerbation of autism argue that they can cause a child sufficient discomfort and distress to disturb sleep, disrupt learning and incite challenging behaviours.

While research into autism and its relationship with food allergies and intolerances continues, what remains beyond question is that proponents construct autism as being physiological/biological and environmental in nature.

Yeast and Candida Causes

Candida is a type of yeast found in the human body, usually in small amounts. However, when the immune system is compromised or damaged, the candida in the gut can overgrow. Advocates of the yeast/candida–autism idea claim that when yeast/candida overgrows in the gastrointestinal tract it too can contribute to the lining thinning and becoming permeable. They hold that this allows the toxins and by-products of the yeast/candida to enter the bloodstream, leading to the behaviours commonly associated with autism. Therefore, the yeast/candida–autism notion is also part of the family of 'leaky gut' theories that are prolific in the field of autism. Furthermore, it clearly belongs within the group of theories that construct autism as being physiological/biological and/or environmental in nature.

Bacterial Infections and Viruses Causes

As with so many of the theories explored in this section, the bacteria/viruses theory is over-arched by the vaccine controversy. The bacteria/viruses theory converges with the vaccine theory in the argument that an immune system dysregulated by bacteria/viruses is further compromised by vaccination. Proponents claim that this renders the immune system unresponsive to the invading measles vaccine, which then migrates to the gut, where it takes up habitation. The argument also proffers that the dysregulation may have been aggravated by a previous bacterial infection that was treated with antibiotics administered without antifungal medication. Antibiotics are known to kill both 'good' and 'bad' bacteria. 'Good' equates with bacteria that can be considered beneficial to humans. Some of these 'good' bacteria maintain the healthy balance of candida/yeast in the gut. Therefore, antibiotics can deregulate the intestinal system, allowing candida/yeast to overgrow.

Once again, this theory clearly belongs within the group of theories that construct autism as being physiological/biological and environmental in nature.

Approaches Stemming from the Ethological Theorists

The Tinbergens, whose ethological theory was looked at in Chapter 2, also favoured therapeutic intervention. Whereas the emotional/environmental theorists took the viewpoint that autism was emotional and environmental in origin, these theorists saw an emotional imbalance within the child as being the cause of the autism. As previously described, they proposed that the nature of this emotional imbalance was excessive anxiety. This excessive anxiety prevented the child from forming normal social bonds with initially the mother, and subsequently others. This then created reservations and inhibitions within the mother, establishing a vicious circle of dysfunctional relations. Therefore, they argued that therapy must be used to overcome the innate anxiety within the child, the built-up bonding difficulties and to provide a context open to bonding.

The therapy they designed received enormous publicity. It was called Holding Therapy. It required the mother to sit with the child facing her on her lap. The therapist then placed the child's arms around the mother whilst the mother held the child's head and attempted to make eye contact with the child. Mothers of older children were sometimes required to lie on top of their children, supporting their weight on their elbows whilst holding their children's heads in their hands. Most children initially put up powerful opposition to being held in this manner. However, even despite received physical assaults, mothers were encouraged to continue trying to establish the longed-for eye contact. Some therapists even insisted on deliberately provoking rage to provide mothers with the opportunity to comfort their children. For example, they removed favourite toys or even frightened children with loud, unexpected noises. Holding sessions were continued until the child relaxed and responded positively to the enforced contact with the mother. At this stage, the focus would shift from the child to the mother, who was then required to examine the inner conflicts she had developed in relating to her child.

Deservedly so, Holding Therapy eventually received much negative criticism. The powerful, emotional nature of this criticism brought with it great public attention. However, here I wish to focus on certain theoretical criticisms because they may offer some guidance into the validity of other, more recent interventions. First, the Tinbergens' theory was that children with autism emotionally withdraw from social interaction because of motivational conflict. Today the commonly held view is that children with autism do not 'understand what is required for social interaction rather than emotionally withdrawing from it' (Roth 1990, p.807). Also, Roth (1990, p.807), reviewing Holding Therapy and its claims of success, found that few of the children participants went 'through a conventional process of diagnosis', adding support to Christie's (1985) criticism that there was a lack of systematic records of success either during or after therapy.

Currently, perhaps partly because of hostile publicity and a subsequent public outcry against Holding Therapy, there are no approaches that openly hold as a core premise the cause of autism as an emotional imbalance within the child. However, it is highly possible that this construction is still held by some individuals who do not understand autism.

Approaches Stemming from the Genetic/Organic Theorists

In many ways, the ideas and studies of the genetic/organic theorists pioneered the current construction of autism as a neurological difference. Also, it is only from their theories that autism can be understood as a difference rather than a disorder. However, it is from the conceptualisations of these pioneers that the behaviourist approaches to autism arose.

Behaviourism

Autism as a genetic difference is fundamentally different from autism viewed as an emotional imbalance within the child and the construction of autism as biological/physiological and environmental in nature. The dissimilarities are most evident in the diagnosis and treatments advocated. In other words, when autism is viewed as an emotional imbalance, relationships, especially significant ones, become the focus, and altering these becomes essential to 'recovery'. Meanwhile, in the construction of autism as biological/physiological and environmental in nature, children with autism are seen to have medical conditions, such as 'leaky guts', mercury poisoning, yeast/candida overgrowths, and so forth. As such, to some extent, these can then be 'treated'. However, in the construction of autism as genetic in nature, the condition is pervasive and life long, and it is in the behavioural interventions and 'management' that change is considered viable.

In many ways, the contrast between these constructions and the approaches they advocate mirrors historical divisions in psychology at the times when these theories were emerging. There are some fundamentally different approaches within psychology. As seen with these varying constructions of autism, what any school of thought within psychology considers appropriate to study is determined by these differences. Briefly, the construction of autism as an emotional imbalance has roots in therapeutic, developmental models in which subjective experience is primary, while the other two constructions have roots in scientific perspectives of psychology, such as the biological and cognitive fields. Where the latter two differ is that the physiological/environmental model primarily envisages post-birth impacts upon the physiological system and the genetic model concerns itself with pre-birth inheritances that determine behaviour from one generation to the next. Therefore, the former investigates the means of alleviating detrimental post-birth impacts, while the latter explores approaches that will reduce behaviours considered outside normal boundaries. The latter has primarily led to behaviourist methods.

Behaviourist approaches include applied behavioural analysis (ABA), the TEACCH approach and the Picture Exchange Communication System (PECS).

Applied Behavioural Analysis (ABA)

The roots of applied behavioural analysis lie in the work and theories of John Watson. In 1913 Watson, reacting against the introspective approach taken by some psychologists, declared that the proper subject matter for psychology was observable behaviour. Moreover, discounting that behaviour was governed by subconscious forces, he stated that all behaviour is controlled by environmental events. From this Watson established the stimulus–response theory upon which the behaviourist movement was founded.

The stimulus–response theory constructs that behaviours are the responses to environmental stimuli. Perhaps the most famous stimulus–response experiment was conducted by Pavlov in 1927, when he paired a bell (the conditioned stimulus) with food (an unconditioned stimulus) and showed that over time a dog would start to salivate (the response) even when the bell was rung without food being present.

In 1938 Skinner differentiated between Pavlov's *respondent conditioning* (conditioned reflexes) and what he termed *operant conditioning* (behavioural consequences control future occurrences), and along with others outlined what became the basic principles of the behaviourist science from which the strategies of *behaviour modification*, later termed ABA, originated. These principles include *reinforcement* (any stimulus that increases the likelihood of a behaviour reoccurring), *prompting* (using stimuli to encourage a person to perform a desired behaviour), *fading* (the gradual reduction of prompts), *shaping* (when a person does not exhibit a desired behaviour, approximations to that behaviour are reinforced in order to gradually establish it) and *schedules of reinforcement* (a set of rules, often termed 'a protocol', that the teacher–trainer follows when delivering 'reinforcers', i.e. desired objects). From these principles, an array of approaches have arisen, such as Løvaas and applied verbal behaviour (AVB).

Also, it is important to note that in a study of verbal operant behaviour Skinner (1957) coined some of the terms still used in ABA today. These include:

- *mand* (a demand reinforced by the delivery and receipt of the 'manded' thing). For example, if a child says 'Want ball', then the ball is immediately given, with the positive reinforcement theoretically increasing the likelihood that the request will be repeated.

- *tact* (a verbal behaviour, including nouns, verbs, adjectives and pronouns, which is controlled by a nonverbal stimulus that is not functionally related to the tact). For example, if a child sees a horse and says 'It's a horse', s/he would be encouraged in this verbal behaviour with a highly desired 'reinforcer'.

Ole Ivar Løvaas

Then Løvaas in the 1960s took these principles and terms, and from them laid out a curriculum of teaching applications/programmes, their training sequences and discussions of how to teach using the science of behaviour. This today is what has become known as ABA, that is, Løvaas's interpretation and application of the principles of behaviourist science.

In it Løvaas first prescribes teaching a target behaviour in isolation and then with one and/or two distractors. Next, another target behaviour is taught in the same way, before both targeted behaviours are randomly rotated as part of the teaching sequence/schedule. Also, in his discussions of how to teach using the science of behaviour, Løvaas placed significant emphasis upon intensity, table-top work, eye contact and sitting still, amongst other strategies.

It is important to note that Løvaas's strategies originally included what were termed *aversives*. 'Aversives' were unpleasant stimuli or responses used to elicit or inhibit behaviours. In other words, they were punishments, such as standing in a corner or a slap to the hand. Possibly pertinent to an age when corporal punishment was considered a normal feature of child rearing and education, these aversives were later removed by Løvaas from all his applications/programmes. That said, Løvaas's (1987) published study, the one often used to promote the effectiveness of ABA programmes by his advocates, is based upon the use of aversives (4 of the 9 in the experimental group, of an overall 19 children who took part in the study, were subjected to slaps to their thighs).

Equally it is important to note that over time the dissemination of Løvaas's work has led to changes. Indeed, in some ways these changes have led to the developments of the TEACCH and PECS approaches outlined next.

Also, perhaps more shockingly to many who would today consider aversives not only archaic but immoral and illegal, a movement has begun towards the use of electric convulsive treatment (ECT) for children/persons with autism since Wachtel *et al.*'s (2008) publication of a case study of a girl with autism and catatonia:

> Recent reports indicate that individuals with autism spectrum disorders have an increased incidence of catatonic symptoms, as well as frank catatonic deterioration. This case report adds support to the limited literature that ECT is a highly effective and potentially life-saving treatment for catatonia in the general population and should figure prominently in the treatment algorithm for catatonic autistic patients as well. A further clinical implication is that autism should be considered in the differential diagnosis as a possible underlying condition in patients seen with catatonia. (Wachtel *et al.* 2008, pp.332–333)

Supporters advocate ECT in the treatment of self-harm behaviours:

> In the past few years, some psychiatrists have stumbled upon a new purpose for the therapy: calming the brains of children with autism who, like Kyle, would otherwise pinch, bite, hit and harm themselves, perhaps fatally. The numbers are small, no more than 50 children treated in the U.S. in any given year, although no one knows the

exact figure. But for this group of children, who are driven by uncontrollable, unrelenting impulses to hurt themselves, ECT grants a reprieve. 'For some of these children who have tried every other treatment modality,' says Kellner, 'ECT can be dramatically helpful and sometimes life-saving.' (Mandavilli 2016, paragraph 8)

Treatment and Education of Autistic and Related Communication-Handicapped Children (TEACCH)

The language used in 'Treatment and Education of Autistic and related Communication-Handicapped Children' is typical of the 1960s in which TEACCH was created. TEACCH started as part of an initiative of the Department of Psychiatry of the School of Medicine at the University of North Carolina, USA. Its aim was to provide services for children with autism and their families. Then, in 1972, the North Carolina General Assembly passed legislation which extended TEACCH to a state-wide community-based pervasive service for children and adults with autism and other similar developmental disorders. Essentially it aspired to provide a systematic, 'cradle-to-grave' service.

Thus, whereas ABA breaks learning down to behaviours to be learnt or reduced, TEACCH assumes a holistic approach to the education and training of children with autism. In doing so, it holds the underlying premise that challenging behaviours may be the result of difficulties with perception and understanding. Also, whilst with ABA parental collaboration is highly prized and behaviour/skills are the focus, TEACCH takes on a whole-environment approach in which the environment is structured to facilitate stress-free understanding, with behaviour modifications generally attended to through environmental adaptations. Therefore, while with ABA children follow individualised education programmes that are regularly assessed and updated to include their emerging skills, with TEACCH modifying the environment to accommodate the needs of children is equally as important as improving strengths and skills.

The Picture Exchange Communication System (PECS)

The Picture Exchange Communication System was developed in 1985 by Lori Frost and Andy Bondy at the Delaware Autism Program. Dissatisfied with the reliance of traditional communication methods upon the teacher, as seen with picture pointing systems and sign language, they sought to develop an alternative system that would enable spontaneous initiation on the part of an individual with communication challenges. In PECS, children are taught to communicate needs through image exchange. This enhances both their communicative skills and understanding of functional communication. It was designed for young and pre-verbal children, and its training practices are based on the principles of ABA. They follow six clearly defined stages.

However, first it is important to note that verbal prompts are not used during the early phases of the system, with the intention of avoiding prompt dependency. To make this possible there is a pre-phase stage at which the teacher/communicator develops an inventory of items the student/child likes. These are known as *reinforcers* and should be highly and consistently motivating to the student/child.

It is also important to note that in the 'training' of phases the system requires a 2:1 ratio of adults to children. This is because PECS requires the teacher/communicative partner to immediately respond to requests and the student/child to initiate, reach for, pick up and hand over images and sentence strips, and at later phases seek out and locate appropriate adults. Therefore, each stage requires a silent facilitator who stands behind the student/child enabling and guiding the targeted behaviours with intentionally decreasing intervention until the phase is independently performed.

Below are the six phases of PECS as outlined by Frost and Bondy (2002).

Phase I: How to Communicate

The objective of this phase according to Frost and Bondy (2002, p.65) is that, 'Upon seeing a "highly preferred" item, the student will pick up a picture of the item, reach toward the communicative partner, and release the picture into the trainer's hand.'

This phase is taught using a single picture selected by the teacher/communicative partner. The phase requires two adults, with one being the communicative partner and the other the physical, silent prompter who facilitates the student/child to reach towards the communicative partner with the picture to exchange in return for the wanted item known as a reinforcer.

Phase 2: Distance and Persistence

The objective of this phase is that 'The student goes to his/her communication board, pulls the picture off, goes to the trainer, gets the trainer's attention, and releases the picture into the trainer's hand' (Frost and Bondy 2002, p.91).

The aim of this phase is that the student/child will persevere with the initiation of a social interaction even when the communicative partner is not close by. Frost and Bondy (2002) compare this to a child without autism raising her/his voice to gain attention when initial attempts have not been responded to. Also, to generalise this behaviour, the phase encompasses training across different settings with a variety of communicative partners and with several reinforcers.

Phase 3: Discrimination between Symbols

The objective of this phase is that 'The student requests desired items by going to a communication book, selecting the appropriate picture from an array, going to a communication partner, and giving the picture' (Frost and Bondy 2002, p.121).

At this stage, the student/child is taught to discriminate between symbols by selecting the symbol which depicts the object they desire. This starts with pairings of pictures portraying preferred and non-preferred items, then moves onto differentiation between two preferred objects, and finally the selection of visual images is increased until the child has an individualised picture book.

Frost and Bondy (2002) devised a step-by-step 'error correction procedure' to be adhered to when a student/child gives the wrong picture. Also, they suggest that for students/children who have difficulty with visual aids, small representative objects are used accompanied by the gradual introduction of pictures. This is like a process known as 'objects of reference', which was developed to assist children who were both deaf and blind to understand, relate and communicate with the external world making use of objects, sounds, smells and tactile sensory experiences. However, as the population using 'objects of reference' has widened, so has its application. They are now considered to have a wider relevance and application to children with additional needs, including children with profound learning difficulties whether they are blind and/or deaf or not. As the name implies, an object is used to represent an activity. For example, a spoon may represent eating, a shopping bag may represent going to the shops, and a pencil may represent time to work with a teacher.

Also, it is important to note that while some students/children continue to use objects as they age, others move on to more visual and, in some cases, symbolic representations, such as photographs, line drawings and common everyday symbols. I note this because, in my opinion, this is in many ways a significant difference between 'objects of reference' and PECS. The purpose of 'objects of reference' is the development of a simple communication system that is founded in an individual's current needs and strengths. Alternatively, the phased approach of PECS appears to imply a push towards furthering current communicative, language and cognitive needs and strengths. In my experience, this can lead to two problems. The first is that a student/child may not move through all the phases but may plateau at one or other of them. This may then be experienced as 'failure', and a blame scenario may ensue. The second problem I have observed is that the phased nature of the system can create a thrust to move through stages before a student/child has profoundly accomplished the objectives set. This can often be seen in the over-reliance upon the silent facilitator as a student/child moves through phases.

Phase 4: Using Phrases
The objective of this phase is that:

> The student requests present and non-present items using a multi-word phrase by going to the book, picking up a picture/symbol of 'I want', putting it on a sentence strip, picking out the picture of what is wanted, putting it on the sentence strip, removing the strip from the communication board, approaching the communicative partner,

and giving the sentence strip to him/her. By the end of this phase the student typically has twenty or more pictures on a communication board and is communicating with a variety of partners. (Frost and Bondy 2002, p.157)

Thus, this phase is designed to teach sentence structure enabling the student/child to make requests using expressions, such as 'I want ___'.

Phase 5: Answering a Direct Question

The objective of this phase is that 'The student spontaneously requests a variety of items and answers the question, "What do you want?"' (Frost and Bondy 2002, p.207).

This phase moves from simply requesting to responding, that is, from 'I want ___' to answering the direct question 'What do you want?', with the target that the student/child will respond whether the desired item is present or not.

Frost and Bondy (2002) contend that Phase 5 skills are quickly acquired because the student/child is by this stage familiar with sentence construction, and being accustomed to want-gratification is strongly motivated to answer.

Also at Phase 5, the student/child is taught 'descriptives', such as colours and sizes. This is designed to enable the student/child to express preferences between similar reinforcers, for example 'I want the red/big ball'.

Phase 6: Commenting

The objective of this phase is that 'The student answers "What do you want?" "What do you see?" "What do you have?" "What do you hear?" and "What is it?" and spontaneously requests and comments' (Frost and Bondy 2002, p.221).

Thus, Phase 6 aims to teach the student/child to move from responding to questions to spontaneously commenting on people, activities and their immediate environment. To achieve this the student/child's database of questions is enlarged to include 'What do you see?'

By the conclusion of all the six phases the expectation is that the student/child will have mastered functional communication skills that include making spontaneous requests, responsive requests, responsive comments and spontaneous comments. However, as stated earlier, in my experience this is not necessarily so as some children plateau at different phases depending on many variables, including cognitive ability, the combination of additional needs and the severity of their autism. Indeed, as 'objects of reference' allow, some students/children may remain at the initial object or picture exchange phase. Hence it has been my experience that the expectation of progression through all the six phases can become the source of frustration and disappointment for parents and professionals alike.

Nevertheless, it was my professional experience that PECS has a rightful place in the interventions available for children with autism, especially the younger learner. I found it to be a useful initial means of teaching the basic elements of communicative exchange and 'requesting', or what ABA terms 'manding'.

Final Thoughts on Approaches Stemming from the Genetic/Organic Theorists

Clearly these approaches share a common construction and directive. First, they all construct autism as primarily genetic in basis. Second, they all seek to reduce behaviours resulting from this genetic inheritance that are considered outside normal boundaries while reinforcing those that are required and acceptable to society.

While to some a focus on observable behaviours either to reinforce or eradicate them is a challenging approach, especially with young children, in my experience it was not necessarily so. If the intervention used is soundly grounded in individual needs and strengths, behaviour modification approaches can prove both successful and rewarding to all involved. In many ways behaviourist approaches simply explain important aspects of learning. For example, the concept of positive reinforcement explains that when a behaviour is followed by a reward then the behaviour is more likely to be repeated. Hence, I suspect that any disquiet in relation to behaviourist approaches is a reaction against those who put method before the individual child. In other words, those who are steeped in one approach to the exclusion of all others apply it rigidly and without digression regardless of the individual needs and strengths of the child/ren they are working with.

Indeed, contrary to some 'good practice' arguments, I used a variety of approaches with every child, some of which may have appeared incompatible to others. For me a structured environment formed the backdrop of my professional practice, whilst knowledge, insight and experience of different approaches was the 'toolkit' from which individualised education plans and programmes could be drawn. No approach was exclusively and rigidly applied, but all could be drawn upon once I had acquired a profound insight into a child's holistic needs and strengths. This included approaches stemming from differing constructions of the nature/origin of autism because my own personal construction of autism as a different, not deviant, way of thinking underpinned and unified my practice. My students were first children with individual personalities who saw the world we shared from a different perspective before they were students with autism.

Note

1. The argument that the preservative thimerosal was used during the manufacturing process of some childhood vaccines to prevent the growth of microbes has been disputed. Contra claims assert that thimerosal was never used in 'live-vaccines', such as the MMR vaccine.

Chapter 4

A CHANGED SOCIO-CULTURE OR IMPAIRMENT INCREASE

Introduction

In this chapter I focus on my conviction that people with autism are not 'impaired' but rather have a different way of perceiving and thinking about the world. Unfortunately, these differences separate people with autism from perceptions and thought processes that the mainstream neurotypical population take for granted. Moreover, as these different perceptions and thought processes can lead to behaviours that are viewed as unusual or unacceptable by a neurotypical-dominated culture, an invisible 'black box' system has emerged (Figure 4.1). In this system the behaviours of people are the inputs to be observed and judged, while the outputs are a range of labels that include us versus them; normal versus impaired; and autistic versus neurotypical.

Furthermore, as autism frequently presents with an additional need, it may have made it easier to view observed differences as 'impairments' of mind. However, in my opinion, the real impairment is located within society and constructions of normality. I believe that in the past, cultural constructions of normality generally nurtured an inability to conceive of difference that was not broken or bad, to be mended, fixed and in some extreme cases criminalised and eradicated. In this I am not denigrating the importance of knowing certain social codes of behaviour for the child with autism, his/her family and the community. This knowledge is often a prerequisite to an independent and fulfilling life. However, a society that could accommodate and adapt to difference without first denigrating it as broken or bad might recognise autism as a spectrum of mind, not disability.

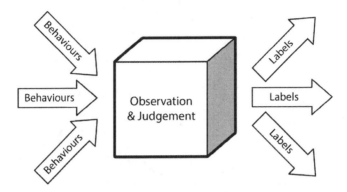

Figure 4.1 Society's 'black box' of behavioural observation, judgement and labelling.

In this chapter I will also explore the now prevalent belief that autism is on the increase, because in many ways I see this as correlational to the viewpoint of autism as a different way of perceiving and thinking about the world. Succinctly put, my argument is that if autism is a different way of perceiving and thinking about the world then it is highly probable that even the subtlest changes in that world will act to exacerbate or reduce the behaviours we now regard to be diagnostic features of autism. In other words, the two contemporary ideas of autism as a different way of perceiving and thinking, and as a growing global phenomenon, are linked for me.

The following issues constitute the substance of this chapter:

- impairment or difference

- increased prevalence or a changing society

- increased prevalence or changes in social constructions of children and childhood

- increased prevalence or changes in socio-educational models[1]

- increased prevalence or changing expectations of developmental stages

- increased prevalence or earlier identification

- increased prevalence or diagnostic changes

- increased prevalence or movement from social entertainment to information technology.

Impairment or Difference

Over-arching this book is the premise that difference does not equate with impairment. Put simply, if one perceives and thinks about the world in a different way to others, then one will relate to it in a different way. Thus although, as previously noted, autism has and is often accompanied by other markers of difference, for example special educational needs, autism itself is essentially a different way of perceiving the external world and processing its sensory inputs. Moreover, the construction of difference implies alternatives, but the label of impairment implies not working properly, bringing with it a host of 'fixing' and 'normalising' connotations.

Look up 'autism and a different mind' and you will be bombarded with articles referring to 'Theory of Mind' (ToM) (see Chapter 1). These all seemingly support the contention that autism is an impairment because the mind of a child with autism is considered incapable or delayed in its ability to empathise with others. From this conclusion comes the imperative of 'fixing' or 'normalising' this incapacity as much as possible. Also, from this conclusion, the focus of intervention is firmly set upon developing the personal and social aspects of empathy, such as turn-taking, co-operation and communication. In other words, we focus upon the very areas that are the 'weaknesses' rather than the strengths of this different mind.

Therefore, in my opinion a construction of autism as an impairment has led to a failure to appreciate both the individual strengths of children with autism and the learning-style strengths of autism generally. The significance of this is critical because learning from the strength of current and emerging skills and abilities is always easier and more profound than learning from where and what we are weak or deficient in. Also, I believe that the construction of autism as an impairment has led to a culture in which the opinions of those with autism can be reasonably overlooked or bypassed because imbedded across societies is the tendency to 'know best' for those labelled impaired or with a 'mental disorder'. This can and has resulted in disregard for their opinions and wishes. Hence today there are adults who, having grown up with autism, are clearly vocalising that interventions addressing their social inclusion were not as important to them as they were to the neurotypical adults teaching them. Some have even stated that they would have preferred help with their sensory processing needs instead.

However, contrary to those who see the 'ToM' as evidence of 'impairment', for me it is evidence of a mind that thinks differently. As outlined in Chapter 1, Baron-Cohen (2003) has developed the idea that a 'different' social cognition is at the core of autism and that, underlying this difference, there may be an 'empathy–systemising' (E–S theory) spectrum that concurs with evolutionarily derived gender differences which ensure the survival and propagation of the species. In other words, the female brain, more predisposed to empathy, tends towards the nurturing and protection of the young, while the male brain, more predisposed to systemising, tends towards the essential order and control of the environment that keeps the familial unit safe. From this viewpoint, Baron-Cohen (2003) proposes that autism is the result of an extreme male brain, which may result from a surge of excessive foetal testosterone hormone during pregnancy. Although I can see how some will construct this extreme male brain as an abnormality rather than a difference, I personally see it as part of a spectrum much as one represented by a bell-curve graph in which the average is only average when extremes at both sides of the curve exist.

Ultimately, I believe that the alteration of the public perception of autism from impairment to difference is our personal responsibility – one person at a time.

Increased Prevalence or a Changing Society

The question of autism's increasing prevalence has in many ways become one of the dominant questions of the day. However, for me it is predominantly a socio-cultural question rather than a statistical or scientific one. To explain my own thinking on this issue I need to refer to the seminal work of the French philosopher and social historian and theorist Michel Foucault (1926–1984).

Michel Foucault (2006 [1961]) proposed that 'madness' is not an innate, unchanging condition but is determined by the socio-cultural structures and thinking of a given society. In other words, Foucault attempted to show how societies construct their definitions of 'madness', or indeed how society constructs madness itself, labelling certain persons exhibiting certain traits, behaviours and/or emotions as 'insane'. For example, female hysteria was once a common medical diagnosis exclusively reserved, as its name implies, for women, but which is today no longer recognised by modern medical authorities as a medical disorder. However, its diagnosis and treatment were routine in Western Europe for many hundreds of years. Indeed, it was widely discussed in the medical literature of the nineteenth century, and women considered to be suffering from it were said to exhibit a wide array of symptoms, including faintness, nervousness, insomnia, fluid retention, heaviness in abdomen, muscle spasm, shortness of breath, irritability and loss of appetite for food or sex. They were also commonly viewed as potential trouble makers to be confined by their families or even removed from society. Clearly 'female hysteria' was not an innate, unchanging condition but one determined by a patriarchal socio-culture that wished to control and limit the role and expectations of women. Hence, as female roles and expectations changed, the condition known as 'female hysteria' disappeared.

So my question becomes, what if autism is not primarily an innate, unchanging 'mental' condition but one determined by neurotypical socio-cultural structures and thinking? In some ways answering my question, Baron-Cohen in 2010 at an autism research conference commented on the fluctuation of 'mental disorders' listed in the *Diagnostic Statistical Manual* since its first publication in 1952. He pointed out that in 1952 the DSM-I contained only 106 'mental disorders', but by its second publication in 1968 the DSM-II contained 182 'mental disorders'. This figure rose again to 265 in the DSM-III (1980), but 'homosexuality' as a 'mental disorder' had been removed. Then in the DSM-IIIR (1987) 'neurosis' was deleted, while the number of 'mental disorders' rose to 292. This figure was reduced to 283 in the DSM-IV (1994). Clearly, as demonstrated by first the inclusion of 'homosexuality' and then its exclusion in 1980,[2] it is possible to conclude that the construction of 'mental disorder' is culturally influenced and interpreted.

Also, again reflecting Foucault's viewpoint, Baron-Cohen (2010) posed the question: 'Are DSM categories just a reflection of socio-cultural biases [and] based on surface behaviour, not biomarkers or causes?'

Clearly diagnosis at present is based on behavioural observations and reports. As seen both with 'female hysteria' and homosexuality, societies and their cultures can label those who are different to the prescribed norms as 'mentally ill or impaired'.

Bearing this in mind, a review of autism as a 'mental disorder' seems appropriate. Hence focusing on its appearance in the US DSM, we find that autism was first included in the DSM-III (1980). Moreover, at that time it was termed 'infantile autism'. However, this name was changed in the DSM-IIIR (1987) to 'autistic disorder', with AS being first included in the DSM-IV (1994). However, in the DSM-5 (2013), the terms were merged into an over-arching autism spectrum, with AS being removed after a short shelf-life of only 20 years. As described in Chapter 2, the resulting new spectrum simply refers to grades of autism: mild, moderate and severe/profound, reflecting now commonly used learning disability terms.

Thus, with both Foucault's view of 'madness' and Baron-Cohen's concern as to the legitimacy of many categories of 'mental disorder', the frequently asked question as to the increase in autism may be seen in a new and very different light: is the sense of increased prevalence a reality or a product of changes in our society and culture?

Increased Prevalence or Changes in Social Constructions of Children and Childhood

I believe that one critical socio-cultural change that has impacted upon the perception of an increased prevalence of autism is how children and childhood are viewed within many societies. I believe that these have led to changes, particularly in Western child-rearing practices, that have had a part to play in the popular impression that autism is on the increase. In the West, we have moved away from the apprentice adult model of child rearing that I was nurtured on. With this model, the child–apprentice adult was expected to know his/her place, demonstrating this by behaving appropriately and submissively in adult company. In my own personal experience, this construction of the child resulted in the co-existence of two very separate worlds. One was the world of the child, ruled over by adults. The other was the adult world on whose periphery children in their own world orbited, knowing one day that they would be admitted to the land of those with 'the say'. Moreover, towards those in the adult world, children were required to abide by common, consistent, unquestionable codes of polite behaviour. Nevertheless, when away from adult supervision, the world of the child was then what we today would consider remarkably free. For example, I remember spending much of my weekends and school holidays away from adult scrutiny from morning to night. I would walk to the park, catch buses and trains, go swimming, visit the cinema, call on and play with friends, and so on. More remarkably, the adults responsible for my care did not seem to worry that I was absent from dawn to dusk so long as my chores were done and I was there for the appropriate mealtimes. Furthermore, I believe that this was a common experience: the norm in child-rearing practices of the day.

Today there is a very different model of child rearing. I believe that this has been influenced by the emergence of individualism and a move away from an external to an internal governance of authority. 'The American dream' of social mobility which invests every individual with the potential of achieving status, influence and prestige has permeated many Western societies. Furthermore, we are daily subjected to this within our own homes. For many hours of every day, television channels broadcast a plethora of reality shows in which ordinary people gain their 15-plus minutes of fame that for a favoured few leads to a life with celebrity status, influence and prestige. Perhaps one of the most famous of these from-obscurity-to-fame television personalities was Jade Goody, who came to public attention via the third series of the reality television programme *Big Brother* in 2002. After her 'eviction' from the programme she went on to host her own shows and to introduce her own products to the public before being diagnosed with terminal cancer.

Jade Goody's story captures the innate promise of individualism which, when coupled with the rise of an internal sense of authority, constructs a very different child model than the preceding one. Today's children are no longer the apprentice adults of yesteryear; instead they have become our future potentialities governed by their parental and familial codes and rules. The difference may seem shallow, but it is not. I was an apprentice adult and, while I understood that my parents wished me to enjoy a better economic life than theirs, their ambitions, rules and codes of behaviour were uniformly in line with all those within our extended family and generally with their entire society, including church, schools, hospitals, clubs and so forth. This shared understanding of social codes and rules of behaviour made it easy for the apprentice child to know what was expected of her/him and how to behave/respond in most situations, and in the case of the apprentice child with autism it can be intuited that if it did not make it 'easy', it certainly made it easier.

On the other hand, the move from common, external authorities to internally idiosyncratic self-governance makes expectations, rules and codes inconsistent and hugely unpredictable. Thus, the individualism of many contemporary societies in reducing shared understanding of social codes and rules of behaviour and nurturing an internal and familial self-governance has produced inconsistent, unpredictable codes and rules that can exacerbate autism. Clearly, in many ways, individualism underpins autism. The very name autism is rooted in the word 'auto' – onto oneself. However, a world with ever-differing rules of social conduct must be immensely confusing, frustrating and frightening to a child with autism. It is also a world which children with mild autism will find it harder to manoeuvre through undetected and undisturbed.

Increased Prevalence or Changes in Socio-Educational Models

Meanwhile Western teaching approaches and methods were also adapting to accommodate the changes in how children and childhood were viewed within many societies. In my opinion, this change also played a significant role in the emergence of the perception that autism is increasing.

As discussed in the previous section, where children were once largely considered miniature adults who were the property of others, they are today, at least theoretically, invested with the rights and freedoms to enjoy childhood and to attain their full potential regardless of their familial and economic origins/backgrounds. Nowhere are these rights and freedoms more powerfully enshrined than in our schools. As Hardyment (1992, p.92) outlined when he wrote 'Since the Second World War, school has become an increasingly important part of a child's life, dominating evenings with homework and effectively ending the old habits of juvenile contributions to domestic management', in many ways, education was the dominant pathway in which the constructions of children and childhood were ultimately changed. Then, as the importance and role of education in the daily lives of children increased, this prompted and enabled changes in the teaching approaches and methods employed in most schools, particularly in the primary sector.

Within my own lifetime what may be termed the 'Piagetian Model' of education, after its founder Jean Piaget (1896–1980), came to dominate approaches and methods used in schools across the globe. Piaget placed great value on the education of children. He did not see them as empty vessels or mini-adults to be environmentally instructed to assume the livelihoods of their forebears, but as creative, thinking beings. He viewed intelligence as part of a maturation process that, with an appropriately stimulated environment, could achieve the highest levels of abstract, cognitive thought. In his developmental model, Piaget argued that intelligence develops in a series of stages that are related to age. He also contended that these stages are progressive, with one stage having to be successfully accomplished before the next can be undertaken, and that each developmental stage carried a construction of reality pertinent to it. For example, at the earliest developmental stage from birth to approximately two years of age, which Piaget termed the 'sensorimotor stage', the child experiences the world through physical movement and the senses, and constructs reality from an egocentric point of view. In other words, children at the sensorimotor stage see the world from a self-centric viewpoint and cannot conceive or perceive of a world from another's point of view.

Piaget also contended that as a child moved from one developmental stage to the next the previous mental abilities acquired are essential in the reconstruction of concepts and reality. This led to an image of cognitive development as an upward, expanding spiral in which earlier ideas were reconstructed based on the higher order concepts acquired at later developmental stages.

However, it is with Piaget's model's reliance upon maturation and the development of sequential cognitive thinking provided the appropriate stimuli are present that I experienced some of my greatest challenges when working with children with autism. For me, Piaget's developmental model constructs a view of children likened unto flowers who need the right nutrients and environments, and, given these, the water, food and sunlight of cognitive development, they will flourish. In relation to this construction, my teaching experiences with children with autism forced me to pose the following questions:

- What happens when a student is light sensitive, has an allergy to the nutrients or needs a different type of soil?

- What happens when because of one of these 'genetic' reactions/ needs, a student cannot imbibe the fertiliser/accommodate it/ assimilate it/or make the necessary adaptation?

As Jasmine Lee O'Neill (2000), a person diagnosed with severe autism, put it in her inspirational book *Through the Eyes of Aliens*:

In Autism, a lot of the assimilation from others in learning isn't present. The children don't automatically pick everything up from parents and teachers. In educating an autistic child in language and communication, it's important to stay aware of this fact. Don't take it for granted that the child will already know what others know. Autistics have a flair for remembering facts and storing knowledge in their brains, computer-style. But they don't usually pick up nuances or common knowledge facts. Something that is not actually learned from a voice or a book is much harder for an autistic to grasp. Rather than fight this fact, go with it. (O'Neill 2000, p.52)

As Piagetian classrooms are supposed to be active, stimulating environments in which co-operative, language-rich learning is encouraged, it is not hard to envisage some of the many challenges they present to students with autism. To quote O'Neill (2000, p.26) again, 'many conversations going on at once will become a confusing blur, as the person with Autism can't process them to decipher their meaning'.

In contrast to Piaget's active, language-based classrooms, Ros Blackburn, who herself was diagnosed with severe autism at a young age, is very clear in her defence of the unflinchingly strict socialisation regime imposed upon her by her parents and the traditional teaching methods of the boarding school she attended. In her address to an audience in Ireland in October 2010 she argued that the explicit rules and consistent codes of social behaviour enforced made learning accessible to her and her social life negotiable. To this contention O'Neill (2000, p.61) adds greater weight with 'Autistics need order and precision to feel safe'.

Thus, the very structures and features of the classrooms I grew up in and moved away from as a young teacher seeking to create a thematic, vibrant, interactive environment aimed at active, language-based learning may be those that reduce stress and provide comprehensible learning and order for students with autism:

> Autistic people aren't jugglers of information, so it is easier for them to be overloaded.

> A large number of autistics have keen hearing. Not only can they detect sounds that are out of the regular person's range; they react to specific sounds in ways others don't.

> Sometimes the voices of other persons can be unbearable to an autistic. (O'Neill 2000, pp.25–26)

Looking more closely at the features of these former classrooms, one finds wall displays that were clearly demarcated from each other and served specific purposes; their very order diminishing visual stimulation. Meanwhile, teacher-directed didactic instruction with a high reliance on book learning was the norm that limited language-based interactions and distractions. Also, the positioning of desks in strict rows all facing the teacher enabled students to work without having to meet the gaze of another student sitting opposite them. Finally, those like myself who were taught in these classrooms will recall that these were places where we knew exactly what was expected and required of us. Moreover, what is even more significant is that these expectations were generally consistently applied throughout the whole school and society, with adults seeming to present a united, agreed front. For example, we all knew to stand when another adult entered the room, to hold doors open around the school for adults and to give up our seats on buses to older passengers. In other words, social codes and norms of conduct, routines and 'rituals (habits)' tended to be consistent across private and public environments, making them less confusing for children with autism and, in the words of O'Neill (2000, p.37), the bringers of 'comfort'.

Furthermore, even some of those working with therapeutic-based approaches, that may seem to have stemmed from the theory of autism as emotional and environmental in origin, have promoted the central place of 'structure' in the education of students with autism. For example, Phil Christie (director of Sutherland House Children's Services, part of the Nottingham Regional Society for Adults and Children with Autism (NoRSACA)), who is an advocate of Intensive Interaction, in a seminar upon this method entitled 'Promoting emotional wellbeing in pupils with ASD' (2010), was very clear that 'structures' should be in place before implementing other interventions and approaches.

Finally, my last argument regarding Piaget's theory is that it does not consider the different effects biological and environmental factors may have depending upon culture and individual characteristics. To consider these in my own professional practice I felt compelled to turn to alternative pedagogical theories, and it was these that guided my mature practice with children with special needs/autism. For example, the developmental social theorists Vygotsky (1896–1934) and Mead (1863–1931) saw interactions with others as central to child development and believed that thought consists fundamentally of internalised social dialogues. Whilst Mead proposed that this internalisation develops through language and role play, Vygotsky accepted Piaget's biological 'natural line' of development but simultaneously proposed another influence that he termed the 'cultural line of development'. The cultural line of development is dependent upon interaction between the child and another person. Vygotsky argued that through this interaction the cognitive functions develop and are psychologically internalised. Equally he suggested that without instruction in abstract sign systems at the 'zone of proximal development' (ZPD), that is, the next step in development, children would not develop purely abstract modes of thought. This argument for buoyed, interactive learning was developed by another developmental theorist, Bruner (1975), who suggested that an adult should supply a supportive but decreasing mental scaffolding. Interestingly this is yet another idea supported by Jasmine Lee O'Neill in her book *Through the Eyes of Aliens* (2000). In it she wrote 'There must be more individualized attention' (p.57).

Furthermore, the argument for what may be described as intensive 'scaffolded' interaction with students with autism is possibly strengthened when one considers that these alternative pedagogical approaches are being recommended for use with neurotypical children. Mead, Vygotsky and Bruner concurred that social and cognitive development are language dependent. Clearly, teaching students for whom language/communication generally requires intervention and adaptation necessitates an increased level of 'scaffolding'. This is most strongly seen in the autism-specific methods that have high adult-to-child ratios. For example, as described in Chapter 3, PECS requires two adults to one child in the initial phase; TEACCH requires one-to-one teaching of new concepts and skills; and ABA and all the intensive play therapies, such as Intensive Interaction and Floortime, require a minimum of one adult to one child.

In the final analysis Piaget's emphasis is on an internal biological development and its process of maturation regarding cognitive development, while Vygotsky and others saw biology as far less important than culture. However, combining both enables a new perspective in which neurological disposition to a certain learning style impacts on how the 'cultural line of development' is delivered to children with autism. For me this directly leads to the need to (1) consider a pedagogy for students with autism, and (2) to further qualify Vygotsky's and Bruner's theories of ZPD and 'scaffolding'.

First, the question of why these developmental theories are valid is emphasised by the additional factor of neurological disposition. In other words, if a student cannot readily assimilate and/or accommodate concepts richly present in a stimulating environment, then the need for a structured, interactive intervention is clearly heightened.

Second, it clarifies 'how' these theories should be implemented in our schools because the neurological disposition to a specific learning style predetermines how the interactive process should be approached in terms of methods, materials and resources. As John Dewey (1859–1952), the American philosopher, psychologist and eminent educational reformist, stated over a century ago, 'the environment consists of those conditions that promote or hinder, stimulate or inhibit, the characteristic activities of a living being' (Dewey 1930, p.13).

Ultimately, I concluded that classroom environments need to be viewed as living organisms, and as such they should alter to suit the needs of students. In other words, classrooms need to adapt and accommodate the different physical, emotional, cognitive, neurological and sensory needs of students rather than students having to fit into pre-existing approaches and structures. For example, when an autism unit I was to work in was being planned, I asked that all classrooms be equipped with an electrical strip that made power points moveable. I explained to the architect that it might be necessary to redesign and reorganise classrooms to suit the individual needs of students. Fixed, unchanging structures are not only unsuitable, but can also be problematic, because environmental inflexibility can be the root cause of challenging behaviours. I am convinced that the combination of rigid structures with a homogeneous teaching approach can exacerbate stress and distress for children with autism. Therefore, without doubt, this is a scenario we should be seeking to rectify.

Meanwhile, many contemporary writers have argued that society now presents greater obstacles to anyone who prefers routine, structured and predictable environments and solitary, focused and linear activities than to those who enjoy more complex, rapidly changing environments rich with opportunities to socially interact and multi-task (Ecclestone and Hayes 2008; Furedi 2003; Moloney 2010; Sennett 1998). Indeed, regarding these challenges, several writers have even questioned the way in which AS has come to be viewed as essentially a psychiatric condition:

> Insofar as such a person failed to conform to the norms preferred by the main economic and political interests that help to shape our lives, then they might come to be seen as 'odd' or even as 'pathological', in time

attracting the attention of educationists and clinicians eager to expand their professional domains in response to parents and other carers, many of whom will have understandable fears that their children will not fit in or might miss out in some way. (Moloney 2010, p.143)

Looking back on my own schooling, I have a sense of a few peers who now would be seen to be 'on the spectrum'. While the child with moderate or severe autism was most likely institutionalised at that time, the child with mild autism probably made it through this more traditional, unaware system, being perhaps labelled 'shy', 'diffident', 'odd', 'idiosyncratic' or even 'peculiar'. For me, the difference lies not with an epidemic of autism but with the gradual emergence of its diagnostic criteria and a correspondingly slow growth in professional and public awareness.

In the 1960s and the early 1970s few people were aware of autism. Indeed, as Silberman (2015, p.41) observed, 'The few paediatricians, psychiatrists, and teachers who read about the obscure condition in a textbook could safely assume they would get through their entire careers without having to diagnose a single case.'

However, this is not to infer an epidemic but an evolution in how autism was recognised and understood. In other words, as described in Chapter 2, research in the field was enabling the construction of autism and its diagnostic criteria to emerge, and as this was happening the awareness of autism and how people with autism may or may not behave was seeping into the public arena.

Nevertheless, awareness was not gradual for all. Some had awareness thrust upon them by having a child with autism but, even then, the professional diagnosis was more likely to be something other, such as 'childhood schizophrenia' or 'mentally retarded'. This was the time before Wing and Gould's (1979) 'Triad of Impairments', and autism as a distinct category was yet to be included in the DSM-III (1980). Nevertheless, even then, awareness for most professionals/teachers was tardy until Oliver Sacks's book *The Man Who Mistook His Wife for a Hat: And Other Clinical Tales* (1985) and the film *Rain Man* (1988) accelerated the development of public awareness. Therefore, I do not agree that this was a time of fewer children with autism, but rather a time of less awareness and greater ignorance. Certainly, for the institutionalised child and his/her peers labelled 'odd' or 'peculiar' in their local schools, I cannot argue that it was a better time or even a better experience.

Increased Prevalence or Changing Expectations of Developmental Stages

One of the most popular theories supporting the viewpoint that autism is on the increase is the controversial MMR debate outlined in Chapter 3. In this chapter I wish to clarify my personal position regarding this argument, that is, that despite all the anecdotal evidence I have heard and read over the years I remain unconvinced that there is a direct, causal relationship between the onset of autism and a child's receipt of inoculation jabs.[3]

However, as with many others working in the field of autism, I am convinced that the developmental stage at which parental awareness acknowledges difference in behaviour is more pertinent than an overnight transformation from a socially articulate child to a withdrawn, non-communicative one caused by a damaging inoculation. For example, it is usually when the parent is moving away from being the dominant interactive partner to the expectation that the child will initiate communication by taking the lead role that the alarm bells are sounded. In other words, as the parent steps back into a more equal communicative interaction, s/he notices that the child does not meet expectations in terms of initiation and response. If we then consider expected behaviours and skills for the early developmental stages relevant to the vaccination of children around their first birthday and then again prior to starting school, how idiosyncratic behaviours and absent skills may start to appear more evident around the time of inoculation becomes clearer.

Usually by six months of age children will do the following:

- turn their head/body towards a sound when they hear it

- be startled by loud, unexpected noises

- watch the face of someone who is talking to them

- show recognition of familiar voices

- smile and laugh when others are smiling and laughing

- make sounds to themselves, such as cooing, gurgling and babbling

- use these sounds to gain attention

- have different cries for different needs, such as one cry for hunger and another one for tiredness.

In relation to children with autism, these milestones may demonstrate why in these early months the identification of autism is masked. For example, the one with significant relevance to children with autism and their parents is the watching of faces of known persons. Whilst children with autism usually avoid eye contact, there may be reasons why a child with autism may choose to watch the face of someone near him/her or who is talking to him/her, as Dr Løvaas (1927–2010), the father of ABA (see Chapter 3), made clear at a conference I attended. He told the story of a young boy with autism who frequently ran away from his class teacher but always seemed to wait to look for her to follow him, almost as though he was taunting her. His teacher, observing his delight in her pursuit, took it personally, to the point that she experienced a sense of deep mortification and offence and turned to Dr Løvaas for advice and assistance. He decided to observe the ritual. During his observations, he discovered that as the teacher chased after the boy little drops of perspiration began to appear on her forehead and gradually run down onto her cheeks. He concluded that it was at these points of immense interest to the child that he stared and derived his delight rather than the chagrin of his teacher as she pursued him daily! In other words, his behaviour carried no calculated ill-will towards his teacher. It was simply a cause-and-effect situation in which the child had learned the following predictable steps: (1) that by running away from his teacher, (2) she would pursue him, and (3) in the pursuit she would perspire, leading to the (4) production of perspiration droplets that (5) he could then stop and watch to his great delight!

With this example, I am suggesting that in the early months of life it is hard to decipher the behaviours of infants, especially for those emotionally involved. It is often the case in life that we see and hear what we wish to and that we may very well continue to do so if we are left to it without impingement from the external world. However, external impingement in the case of children with autism may be seen to be developmental. Within months of the first quite general milestones, more exact and less easy to misread ones will expectantly be looked for.

The next developmental milestones that should be in place before a child usually undertakes an autism assessment occur around 18 months of age. By this time children will usually do the following:

- understand a few simple, frequently used words, such as 'drink', 'car' and 'cup'

- have a vocabulary of approximately 20 of these simple, frequently used words, such as 'book' and 'dog'

- understand a few simple, frequently used phrases, such as 'give me', 'clap hands' and 'kiss mummy'

- demonstrate this developing understanding by pointing to familiar people and objects, such as 'daddy' and 'car'

- also from this developing understanding, use language in a more recognisable way, such as using words (verbalisation) to gain attention rather than simply using sounds (vocalisation)

- alongside increasing verbalisation, use gesture or pointing, often with words or sounds (vocalisation) to show what they want

- copy things adults say and gestures they make

- show enjoyment for games, such as 'peek-a-boo' and 'round-and-round the garden'

- demonstrate enjoyment for toys that make noises

- start to show enjoyment for pretend play, such as pretending to eat imaginary food or to talk on a play phone/mobile.

Clearly some of these milestones are in sync with behaviours associated with autism. These include copying things adults say and demonstrating enjoyment for toys that make noises. However, while a young child who is learning to talk is expected to repeat the speech of others, meaningless repetition of heard spoken words is one of the diagnostic behaviours of autism known as echolalia. Therefore, while parent/s and/or carer/s may delight in a child's ability to copy things adults are saying around them, with a child with autism they could be witnessing the first instances of echolalia. Equally, as many children enjoy toys that make noises, this common thrill may turn out to be a behaviour associated with autism. Therefore, even at this second developmental stage, the diagnosis of autism may prove difficult and this may explain why some parents experience the onset of autism as being post two years of age following the MMR vaccination.

The next significant developmental stage occurs between 18 months and two years. If autism is suspected this may coincide with an autism assessment. At this stage, children generally do the following:

- exhibit longer periods of concentration when engrossed in activities, such as playing with a favourite toy

- engage in pretend play with toys, such as feeding teddies or pretending to drive a car

- sit and attend to simple picture stories

- copy sounds and repeat words a lot

- understand approximately 200–500 words

- use a limited number of sounds in words (these are usually 'p', 'b', 't', 'd', 'm' and 'w');[4] however, they will also usually omit the endings of words, only speaking audibly about 50 per cent of the time

- use approximately 50-plus, increasingly recognisable, single words in speech

- begin to put simple sentences with two to three words together, such as 'bye Daddy', 'more juice' or 'go car'.

In many ways, the changes observed between the second and third developmental stages represent an accelerated movement from egocentric to social beings. Also, at this stage, adults generally have an increasing expectation of children's communicative initiation and reciprocation. Therefore I would argue that the widening gap between the communicative and social skills of a child with autism and a neurotypical child, coupled with the increased expectations of carers, magnifies what may have been previously hidden by adult initiation and dominance in interactions.

Increased Prevalence or Earlier Identification

Progress in autism awareness and recognition is enabling earlier and greater identification of autism. This includes those with mild autism who may have previously gone unnoticed because of coping strategies and skills. However, I believe that as we have become more proficient in the diagnosis of autism we have naturally widened the ratio of people with autism, and that this has also contributed to the belief that autism is on the increase. In other words, it is not autism per se that is on the increase but simply our ability to recognise and identify it.

The earlier the identification of autism is made, the more the neurological construction of autism as a different functioning mind is supported, and the idea that autism is caused by the MMR vaccine may be further ruled out. At present, autism in children is diagnosed from two years of age on into the teenage years using behavioural checklists. However, clarification in diagnostic behaviours are enabling observational identification at earlier and earlier ages. Indeed, some researchers are now arguing that indications of autism can be seen in subtle differences in the attention to faces given by babies only a few months old. For example, a study carried out with infants as young as six months old found that those who go on to develop autism not only looked at faces less than other babies, but they also showed a tendency to look away from important facial features when someone spoke (Shic, Macari and Chawarska 2014).[5]

Increased Prevalence or Diagnostic Changes

In my early twenties, I was honoured to know David and Althea Brandon. They were the inspiration behind my professional life because they modelled and taught me the value of living an empathetic, compassionate life. In doing so they encouraged and nurtured my passionate concern for social justice and equality. They did this by giving me a home and inviting me to join them in their many efforts to enable people with learning disabilities and mental health needs to live 'normal' lives. Indeed, David was one of the UK's pioneers of the earliest form of inclusion, termed 'normalisation'. They had an open house, understanding hearts and warrior spirits but without the artifice and pretence of detached or overbearing 'niceness'. Althea's words and actions had a depth of reflective consideration that I envied. She knew how to stand back and consider options and actions. Meanwhile David was one of the most angry and passionate people I have ever had the honour to meet. He went to war with injustice, inequality and inhumanity. As a couple, they were an almighty team. As a team, they were the catalyst for change in the lives of many, directing their united passion, anger and struggle for change towards improving the well-being of people with learning disabilities and mental health both on an individual and a general level. Towards this end, David worked tirelessly even in the last days of his brief, remarkable life.

It is from my journeys with David that I arrived at the argument that autism appears to be more prevalent partly because of contemporary diagnostic changes. These journeys took me to some of the large institutional establishments usually situated on the outskirts of our cities and towns. To me they were places where we could house and hide those who society did not know how to accommodate and include – people who differed from our narrow definitions of 'normal'. At the time when I was making these visits neither the diagnosis nor understanding of autism had been honed. Therefore the predominant diagnosis made was one relating to a learning disability. If the learning disability masked autism, few were looking and fewer still were interested. Also, it may be true to say that behaviours now related to autism were seen to exist because of the predominant learning disability.

For me today we have travelled 180 degrees, because when the diagnosis of autism is given, few look beyond it to ascertain the dominant need/s of a child despite recommendations of good practice that argue for this. One such recommendation can be found in the Irish *Report of the Task Force on Autism* (2001), which states:

> Clearly, factors in addition to a clinical diagnosis of an autistic spectrum disorder will need to be included in determining the degree and nature of a person's special educational needs... The severity of the ASD will, therefore, play a role, as will any additional disabilities... For all persons with an ASD, it is likely that they will have special needs, which will require additional and special educational provision to be made. (Government of Ireland 2001, p.25)

I am not saying that a holistic assessment of need is not considered or undertaken. I am saying that, once the diagnosis of autism is suspected or given, any assessment undertaken under the umbrella of autism colours the subsequent educational provision recommended and provided. Hence, in my own experience, I have worked with children with autism whose dominant needs were not within the autism remit. For example, there were children whose dominant needs were situated within the severity of their learning disability. Their dominant needs did benefit from the well-structured, task-oriented, clear goals of the autism class they were assigned, but their progress in it was not the same as peers whose dominant needs were situated within their autism. Also, for many parents and professionals, addressing their autism became the predominant, at times misleading, occupation. In this way I came to believe that, where a learning disability had once masked autism, autism has come to mask other special educational needs. Therefore for me autism should not be a one-size-fits-all diagnosis, as an individual's prognosis is often dependent on their additional needs. Also, how these are met should be filtered through the lens of individualised profiling.

Increased Prevalence or Movement from Social Entertainment to Information Technology

This section addresses the eclipse of social entertainment by the waxing phenomenon of information technology. The key for me is the disappearance of the word 'social' and the arrival of the word 'information'. Social implies communication and interaction between persons, but information is simply the acquisition of what can be known.

There are many who will forcefully argue that the internet enables the isolated and lonely to access communication and company. For example, at a conference on successful aging that I attended in 2014, one presenter spoke of her success with internet communication aimed at elderly participants who live on their own. However, her research also revealed that participants listed most highly the desirability of a website where they could contribute their skills and expertise to others, and that those who had benefited from increased internet access still bemoaned the loss of home visits from medical/social service staff. For me internet communication, though preferable to nothing else, is still the black-and-white version of social interaction when compared to the HD colour of the thing itself. The elderly participants referred to in this research were clearly not fooled either.

But what of our young, the children growing up in this new technological age in which information and communication is easily and readily accessed through devices to which many of us seem continually attached? In homes and schools across continents children with or without autism now spend significant periods of time engaged with technological activities that, in my opinion and understanding of autism, are encouraging, reinforcing and promoting behaviours we have come to associate with autism.

Looking closely at those who have made significant contributions towards this information revolution illuminates my argument even more. For this I turn again to the research of Baron-Cohen. In a presentation given at a Research Autism conference in 2012, he described research undertaken into the ratios of children with autism born to fathers who worked in the so-called 'Silicon Valley' of the USA. The results found a 50 per cent higher ratio. Moreover, when repeated in two areas of Europe where male employment is traditionally and predominantly in the technology and engineering fields, the findings were consistently the same.[6]

What suppositions can we make from this? Some may call the following presumptions rather than suppositions, but within my own practice I struggled with the heavy reliance some parents and professionals would place on the daily use of technology. Their arguments for this extended from a simple regular motivator to the means of teaching new concepts and strategies. Also, it was often advocated as being the most powerful and engrossing de-stressor for child, family and others sharing the environment with the child. Except for how we teach new concepts and strategies, I do not wish to disagree with any of these arguments. I agree that access to information technology is a strong motivator for many children with autism, and as such it can provide a much-needed respite for the child and those responsible for him/her both at home and in school. However, predominantly designed by minds that tend towards the systematic rather than the empathetic – or put more pertinently to this argument, towards information gathering rather than communicative interaction – ultimately what computer technology is doing is promoting and reinforcing a style of thinking and behaving we have labelled as autism.

To expand upon this, I must add that the argument I am making did not arise from these reported findings. These findings simply supported and made sense of observations made within my classroom practice. These observations were:

- When working on a computer, children usually sit facing a wall with their backs to others.

- When working on a computer, children are in control of any communication process it may involve. For example, they can stop the communication, fast forward or repeat it as they wish.

- Computer software and programs tend to encourage repetition of behaviour and consistency of outcome.

- Even when aimed at teaching social skills, computer software and programs are stilted and repetitious. The unexpected, which occurs frequently in human-to-human communication, appears to be still beyond the programmable.

Nevertheless, Baron-Cohen's (2012) reported findings offer us clear evidence that amongst the pioneers and engineers of the technology we readily expose our children to are many with autism-like characteristics and/or tendencies. Therefore it is easy to suppose that the creations of the intelligent and logical minds that lead and develop the information technology field mirror the minds that created them. Furthermore, this implies that these valued inventions are nurturing thinking and behaviours we attribute to those on the autism side of humanity's spectrum, such as rigidity of thinking and repetitious behaviours. In other words, socialisation is not a realistic remit of a computer program. Instead socialisation along with communicative skills and strategies must remain firmly and irrevocably the remit of human-to-human contact and interaction. This means that computer programs may through consistent repetition reinforce socialisation concepts and skills which have been taught person-to-person, but they cannot adequately teach the intricacies and complexities of socialisation given the cut and thrust of actual human communication.

To this I hasten to add that I did and would again use computer technology in my classroom. It truly motivates and de-stresses children with autism. However, its use was and should always be deeply considered and personalised because of its innate 'autistic' nature. Additionally, I wish to state that I did not and still do not construct it as a teaching tool for new concepts, especially concepts of socialisation. As a teaching tool, it is best used to practise and reinforce concepts already taught human-being-to-human-being.

Notes

1. I use the term socio-educational to emphasise that these models, although based on academic child developmental theories, are primarily social in nature and it is their pervasive cultural penetration that has encouraged educational change.

2. As a point of interest, the DSM-II (1968) was published by the American Association of Psychiatrists a year after the enactment of the Sexual Offences Act (1967) in England and Wales. This Act decriminalised homosexual acts in England and Wales between two men in private when both were over 21 years of age. However, in 1968 the American cultural landscape regarding homosexuality was still a patchwork of divided opinion in which the dominant mindset remained anti-homosexuality.

3. Regarding the MMR vaccine controversy and my opinion that there is no causal relationship between the vaccine and autism, I will concede that there is always an exception to any rule. If you are convinced that your child's autism stemmed directly from such an inoculation, your child may well be the exception. Even if this is so, this chapter may yet have insights into the prevalence of autism that may better aid you to meet your child's learning style and needs.

4. 'p', 'b', 't' and 'd' are known as the short plosives or stops. They are all produced at the front of the mouth – 'p' and 'b' by the lips, and 't' and 'd' by the ridge behind the teeth. 'm' is a nasal sound and 'w' is known as an approximant. Both are also produced at the front of the mouth and, like 'p' and 'b', by the lips.

5. Dr Shic, who co-wrote the 2014 study, is a member of the Autism Speaks Baby Siblings Research Consortium (BSRC) that brings together various research teams

from around the globe with the intention of discovering the earliest predictors of autism.

6. Baron-Cohen (2012) acknowledged that, given the traditional division of labour in the 'Silicon Valley' workforces with men in the workplace and women in the home, research into the ratios of children with autism born to mothers working in these areas was yet in its infancy.

PART II

UNDERSTANDING THE THEORY OF AUTISM AS DIFFERENCE IN PRACTICE

Chapter 5

SCHOOL AND CHILDREN WITH AUTISM

Introduction

The aim of this chapter is to give an overview of the ingredients I believe make for a successful schooling experience for children with autism. I base these on my actual teaching practice both within mainstream classes and classrooms specially dedicated and designed for children on the autism spectrum.

A School for All

So, what does a school need to fittingly serve children with autism and their visual learner peers?

In the first instance, a school should have a clear vision aiming to create a safe, calm and friendly environment that is conducive to the learning of students and the well-being of all. The end of that statement is not a mere adage. It is the staple point. Too often in contemporary schools, now transformed for all intents and purposes into mini-business projects, staff are required to treat parents and children with a respect and consideration not institutionally shown to them. The roles of classroom teachers and support staff are now more akin to that of sales personnel selling the product 'education' in competition with other neighbouring schools while managed by bosses driven by financial considerations. This has created a serious division of practice in which teachers and support staff are asked to output large degrees of respectful compassion and understanding while inputting a sense of institutional disregard for their own well-being. The large, institutional 'white elephant' being clearly ignored is that how we treat those who work and care for others will eventually affect how they professionally and personally perform their duties and responsibilities. Indeed, we are living through times marked by internationally high rates of teacher attrition, especially in the sector of special education, and it is more those who persist within the field who contradict the trend than those who leave after a few years. Clearly, in the field of autism where experience is an advantage to children, parents and all concerned, workers need a safe, calm and friendly environment conducive to their best work with students. As on aeroplanes in which carers are reminded to put on their own oxygen masks before attending to those of others, only when the carers are provided for can the needs of the children in their care be well met.

Moreover, creating a safe, calm and friendly environment that is conducive to the learning of students with autism requires a profound knowledge of all their educational needs and thorough intervention addressing these. It also requires knowledge and acknowledgement of the strengths of individuals, respect of differences, and celebration of the efforts, learning and the smallest steps of progress of students, staff, parents and all concerned. However, none of these are achievable without a sense of teamwork in which communication, co-operation and collaboration between staff, students, parents and external professionals exists, and in which responsibilities are shared, decisions agreed are supported, and conflicts or blame are avoided.

Finally, a school fit for a child with autism does not forget the individuality and diversity of all its students, and to do so it recognises the need for staff to vigilantly and positively self-reflect. Therefore, it encourages staff to question their preconceptions to avoid rigid, unrealistic and limited demands and vision of/for students, others and, importantly, themselves. Also, it aims to enable each individual student to develop to his/her fullest, independent potential academically and personally acquiring socially necessary life skills. Ultimately, in a school fit for a child with autism, each individual student, parent, teacher, support staff and all involved persons are treated as valued human beings.

Then, beyond such a profound depth of vision and intention, a school fit for a child with autism adopts certain guidelines and practices that facilitate the creation of a safe, calm and friendly environment that is conducive to the learning of students and the well-being of all. These guidelines and their practices ensure that classrooms are attuned to the needs and strengths of all, not just children with autism. As such they are guidelines and practices applicable to all, not just the teacher and the child with autism but all staff, all students, all parents, all external professionals and others.

Guidelines and Practices for Schools Fit to Serve Children with Autism (and Visual Learners)

The following are 12 essential guidelines and accompanying practices that all who work with children with autism should know and adhere to. They are key to the happy and successful schooling of children who mostly see the world from a very different perspective than those in whose care they are placed. They are also helpful to parents and other carers as they relate to the common needs of children with autism in home and play environments. Finally, most importantly, to be effective they should all be underpinned by home and school working co-operatively and collaboratively together with an endless degree of goodwill based upon mutual respect. In stating this I urge all parents/carers and professionals to abandon blame and recriminations, to see each other as human beings with good intentions, all working towards the best educational provision possible for a child, all burdened by their own responsibilities and demands and not all-knowing experts. Additionally, for our children with autism, I would ask all parents and professionals not to see them as defected or impaired but, as Henry David Thoreau (1854) wrote, as young people walking to the beat of 'a different drummer': not to be cured but to be enabled and inspired by their educational experiences.

Whole School Approaches

The child with autism needs a certain level of consistency. However, as codes and rules of behaviour in our modern world have become progressively individualised, it is now not uncommon for all children to be confronted and confused by discrepancies between familial and societal expectations, and even marked differences between the expectations of different classroom teachers. While neurotypical children may adapt to these with little or no stress and distress, the child with autism more than likely will not. Therefore, there is a significant need for schools to adopt whole school approaches, especially regarding codes and rules of behaviour. Ultimately, in my opinion, this would be advantageous to all children.

The codes and rules of conduct/behaviour should be few but they should be consistently applied throughout the school. While they should have long-term relevance to the social world, it must be borne in mind that children with autism may interpret them literally and rigidly, so setting in stone any rule or code of behaviour that you may need to change later is unadvisable. Finally, as much as possible, they should take a positive, rather than negative, approach in which required behaviours are clearly stated as opposed to denouncing inappropriate ones.

Also, there needs to be a whole school approach to supporting these codes and rules of conduct/behaviour with visual aids. Unfortunately, some adults do not recognise or understand the significance of such measures. In my practice I was often challenged by the argument that a certain child with autism was high functioning and therefore understood everything that was being said. However, with some of these children, as I observed them in home and/or school situations, they were clearly edging towards 'meltdown' while the attending adult repetitively endeavoured with an overdose of language to prompt or direct the child. Observing these incidents, I concluded that this was disrespectful to autism and its learning style because it was tantamount to saying that the visual presentation of information is somehow inferior to the auditory. It is not. Let us not forget that in the past many of us used diaries or calendars to remind ourselves of forthcoming meetings, dates or events. Then there were the 'yuppie'-friendly filofaxes. Now we have our mobile phones and laptops with visual reminders constantly popping up. If the neurotypical mind, with all its auditory abilities and strengths, needs such visual aides-mémoires, then there can be no argument against supporting children with autism to recognise and remember codes and rules of behaviour with visual signs.

Thus, a school fit for a child with autism would recognise the need for rules and codes of behaviour to be visually displayed. While these should be positive, directing children toward the preferred behaviour/action, in my experience there are three visual aids that are needed on a whole school level to support and promote the wider school codes and rules. These must-haves are signs for waiting, turn-taking and stopping. As well as being used with individual children who need to develop the behaviours named, they are invaluable when placed in appropriate places around a school. For example, I have used the 'waiting' sign on doors to prevent children walking in or out unsupervised. Also, I have used it when waiting in queues, crossing roads and even on toilet doors when teaching individual children to knock and wait for a response instead of barging into an occupied but unlocked cubicle. As to the turn-taking sign, it is a great reminder for all children and is useful when included as an essential part of any turn-taking game, especially with young children. Finally, the stop sign has often seemed to me, and those I have encouraged to use it both in homes and in schools, to have magical properties. I have placed it on cupboard doors, drawers, room doors, equipment and literally anywhere it was not advisable for children to have unsupervised access and, as though by magic, few trespassed.

In conclusion, some whole school practices arising from whole school approaches are:

- whole staff awareness to reduce auditory input to a minimum when a child with autism is going into or is in crisis

- the use of agreed visual aids/signs for waiting, turn-taking and stopping

- visual schedules appropriate to each class displayed in every classroom throughout the school

- visual rules and codes of behaviour appropriate in style and presentation to each class displayed in every classroom

- consistent teacher expectations in relation to how children behave in specific, common situations, for example response to greetings, questioning, turn-taking and waiting

- consistent teacher strategies in relation to working with children with autism – for example, when giving instructions/expecting student to absorb information, sit them close facing the adult talking; when asking a question of a student, address them with their full name before asking question; use visual aids and objects to explain ideas/concepts; come down to child level when talking, especially when asking questions or reprimanding; and provide child/class/age-appropriate countdowns to end activities that respect the need to prepare for transition from one task to another.

De-Stress Strategies/Practices

A school fit to serve all children with autism would be aware of the generic causes of stress and distress to them, and have in place approaches and practices to extinguish or reduce these. These should include:

- A whole school policy that values and encourages the use of visual aids and kinaesthetic approaches in the teaching of new skills and concepts and recognises the need for increased preparation and practice for unfamiliar events with increased visual and kinaesthetic elements to these rehearsals.

- All staff being aware that they should reduce speech/communication when a child with autism appears agitated or in crisis. Also, alongside the need to reduce speech/communication when a child with autism is agitated or in crisis, training and equipping staff to use basic visual aids at these times would benefit all. For example, visual aid cards for stop, wait and turn-taking could be productively used throughout a school to prevent and defuse challenging situations.

- All classrooms displaying age/ability-appropriate class timetables/schedules that progress from objects of reference through pictorial images/representations to written subject headings as children age and become literate. These enable the child/ren with autism to have the comfort of knowing when their least preferred lessons will end and when their preferred lessons will be.

- Countdown to end activities with visual aids, for example using dice/number cards or sand timers with younger, less able children, and clocks or kitchen timers with older, more able students.

- A quiet working place (workstation) in every classroom where a child who needs limited visual stimulation can choose to go or be regularly directed to for their independent work.

- Keeping some areas of classrooms blank or very plain, such as the walls children face when working.

- Label at child-appropriate heights all rooms, areas, facilities, activities and so on.

- Demarcate areas to enable child/ren with autism to concretely understand the requirements and purposes of different areas and their subjects, for example art and craft, play and class library.

- Label books with subject headings as well as names.

- Store books in subject piles with each pile clearly subject labelled at child height.

Beyond these, one of the most essential strategies is the provision of stress-free interludes and places. Children with autism need these as much as their neurotypical peers need playtime. In my opinion, children with autism are some of the bravest people one can meet. Imagine waking up every day to a confusing world filled with incomprehensible requests and commands, overwhelming sights and sounds, and unpredictable rules and codes of behaviour. Imagine having to engage with that world in which avoidance of social norms and/or inappropriate behaviours can escalate at any given moment into one of crisis. Imagine being persistently pressured by the beings of that world to partake with them in conversations, interactions and exchanges that are meaningless, frustrating and stressful for you. Imagine being required to make eye contact with those beings in whose eyes your distress is exacerbated. To further elaborate this point, consider the following scenario. It is a generic description that reflects observations of several children during my years of practice:

> In a brightly decorated, language-rich reception class sits a small boy at a group table, two tables away from his teacher. He sits facing other students. To look at his teacher, he must turn his head right and look past several other heads and possibly pairs of eyes. He appears highly stressed. He waves his hands and arms about, and spends a lot of his time repeating words and phrases from television programmes. When addressed directly, his head goes down, his movements become more agitated and his echolalia increases. To assist him to fit into the classroom's practices, routines and curriculum, without causing distress to self and others, the school has acquired an assistant. She sits next to him. She is there to constantly bring him back to the external world and to ensure he interacts with it. She is there to ensure he completes tasks. She is even there on the playground requiring him to play with peers. There is no place in the whole school where he can escape like any other student into his own reverie.

While neurotypical children de-stress on playgrounds running around interacting with peers, children with autism can experience their greatest stresses and distresses in their noisy breaktimes when all seeming order and predictable routines are suspended. If, at these times, demands are made upon them to interact with others in ways that may have no meaning for them, breaktimes can become nightmarish. Clearly children with autism need a different type of relaxation and release.

In my last teaching post, I was fortunate enough to be able to provide a break area equipped with toys and other resources that I had observed individual children choosing to occupy their free time with. These included shopping catalogues, personalised photography albums, Disney character figures and small cars. Also, the area was well equipped with comfort resources, such as small tents, cushions and soft blankets. Most importantly, in this area no adult put any pressure upon a child. Staff were instructed not to engage in any interaction with a child unless addressed by a child directly. It was the children's own place for de-stressing, and to a child with autism this usually means going into their own non-verbal world with objects/toys of their own choosing.

However, the safety of the area required proactive planning. This included scheduling children to use it in shifts and paying attention to children who could not be near or with other/s for various reasons. Furthermore, the area required careful maintenance. As it was a stress-free zone for children, the usual tidy-up requirement was suspended unless a child wished to keep a favourite toy/object in a special place. Hence maintenance was the responsibility of staff who had to wait until the area was vacated so as not to bring stress into this place of sanctuary.

A Sense of Place/Belonging for All

A school fit to serve all children would provide every child with a sense of place and belonging, especially those with autism. For the younger child this is easily enabled with a photographed and labelled desk, clothes peg, locker and so on. For the older student I would recommend encouraging him/her to personalise their own places/spaces. For example, some of my older students created their own decorative labels while others decorated labels I provided. Some adults may think this practice inappropriate for some older students. However, it was never my experience that even the older student found the demarcation of their own personal place and space within the classroom inappropriate or unwelcome.

Significantly there is an extra bonus to creating individual places/ spaces for children with autism in classrooms. This is the enormous independence it gifts the child/student. I have seen very young children with moderate and severe autism and additional needs purposefully enter a classroom, hang up their outer clothing on their labelled peg, put their lunch box in their own labelled pigeonhole and then walk over to their labelled/photographed desk to read and follow their individual schedule – all without supervision, assistance or prompting. Standing back and observing these children moving effortlessly and decisively without any intervention or support has quite simply been one of the joys of my life.

Speech Reduction

One of the most important guidelines/practices when working with children with autism is to reduce speech, keeping it to a minimum, especially in a crisis. Children with autism all have some level of difficulty with auditory processing, that is, the auditory modality. These difficulties can include one or many of the following:

- an inability to screen out or differentiate sounds

- over-loading

- miscomprehensions or a limited comprehension

- ability diminishing as stress increases, making auditory processing the least reliable modality in stressful situations.

I am aware that there are children with mild autism for whom this advice may seem irrelevant, but I strongly believe that this thinking is mistaken. By the nature of the diagnosis there is the premise that the child has some difficulty with language and social communication, and both are predominantly the domain of auditory processing. In my teaching practice I knew children with AS, now referred to as mild autism, who were fluent speakers and apparently competent in their understanding of the spoken word, yet they struggled to follow verbal instructions, make sense of verbally taught concepts and comprehend conversational requests. Had their needs not been understood and instructions, concepts and requests not been presented in clear, visual formats alongside concise and precise verbal inputs, these difficulties could have led to or exacerbated frustrations, learning difficulties, behavioural issues and other problems.

Visually Aid and Clarify

It is one of my curious speculations that in the past many teachers were auditory learners who because of their own predisposition taught predominantly using the auditory modality. Today, while different learning modalities and needs are recognised and understood, in many classrooms there is still a respectful weightiness shown to auditory learning. This is particularly seen in the terms of an emphasis placed upon listening and speaking skills. Furthermore, this focus is promoted by educational theories that advocate language-rich environments in which activity-based, participatory learning occurs. Although the activity base makes allowances for kinaesthetic/hands-on/tactile/ motor learning, for children with autism the accompaniment of participatory language-based interaction with others can prove an anathema. For children with autism and visual learners experiencing some level of difficulty with the auditory modality, an alternative, whole school approach is called for.

This approach includes the stress-reducing strategies/practices listed in 'De-Stress Strategies/Practices' above, with a focus upon enabling and enhancing comprehension, learning, emotional well-being and appropriate social behaviour using visual aids. Significant amongst these aids are visual schedules, with all aids and schedules being appropriate to the child, that is, 'objects of reference', photographs, pictures, icons and the written word.

However, I believe that it is important to stress that visual aids and schedules are not 'cures' for autism. They are learning enablers that are compatible with the visual learning style of children with autism. Unfortunately, during my years of practice, I did hear some professionals infer that if a certain approach or method was carefully adhered to a child with autism would progress through the spectrum of visual aids as through developmental stages: 'objects of reference', photographs, pictures, icons and the written word. In my experience this is not always true. For example, some children continued to use a combination of pictures-with-words or icons-with-words throughout their primary schooling. Therefore, it is important to bear in mind that learning ownership, understanding and de-stressing are the remits of visual schedules, not necessarily upward progression.

Also, a visual schedule must be based on the individual child's abilities and competencies. Clearly, there are many factors to be considered when deciding upon the type of visual support a child is given and when this support needs to be changed or not. These factors are, and always should be, individual to the child. They include cognitive ability and any other additional educational need/s a child may have. Therefore, in the initial base-line assessment, undertaken by a teacher as a child with autism is placed in their care/classroom, consideration of the appropriate visual aid structure to support the child's learning and well-being is essential.

Nevertheless, regardless of individual differences, especially in the early years as a child assimilates spoken and written language, I believe that it is essential to support verbal instructions and requests with visual cues, such as cards for 'stop!' and 'wait!' (Figures 5.1 and 5.2).

*Figure 5.1 Visual aid supporting request to stop
or not to venture in or beyond.*
*The cross is drawn in red, reflecting the stop stage of the traffic light
sequence. The word 'NO' is written in black and capital letters.*

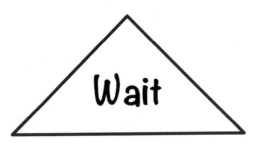

Figure 5.2 Visual aid supporting request to wait.
*The background is yellow, reflecting the amber stage of the traffic
light sequence. The word 'Wait' is written in black.*

Equally, I believe that we should not make premature, rigid assumptions about what any child can or will learn. Therefore, the written word should either be part of the visual aid or an alongside accompaniment.

Also, as transitions can be challenging, visual timetables can assist children with autism through them, and should be maintained per a child's needs. Simultaneously, visual timetables assist comprehension and literacy skills by associating events with pictures and words. They also reinforce a sense of the movement of time as they encourage children to vary activities and interests (Figure 5.3).

Monday	🏠	School	
Tuesday			
Wednesday			
Thursday			
Friday			
Saturday	🏠	Home	
Sunday			

Figure 5.3 An example of a visual timetable.
This timetable simply depicts school days and weekends.

Visual timetables can also promote personal and social well-being reducing behavioural difficulties. First, they enable children to see when their preferred activity is scheduled. Second, they remind them that the task they least prefer has a clear start and will have a definite end (Figure 5.4).

Figure 5.4 An example of a visual timetable.
This shows the child a clear start, end and flow to activities,
culminating in a preferred 'reinforcer' activity.

However, as stated above in 'Speech Reduction', this approach is not without its critics, who predominantly find fault with its use with older students. I am bemused by this opinion because I know few adults who do not have mental or written/text time-relevant plans and/or meetings to which they try to adhere. For example, most professionals use some means of reminding themselves of their schedules and important events/meetings, such as diaries and mobile phone reminders. Also, in the case of older students, there are always timetables or schedules to follow. Impressively, some of the primary age children I worked with were successfully reading and interpreting timetables appropriate to secondary school age students by the time they left my classroom, that is, word only, top-down lists of work activities they were expected to complete that day and/or that week.

Table 5.1 is an example of a weekly timetable like those I have known young children with autism follow without any prompting.

Table 5.1 A visual timetable showing a weekly schedule.

Time	Monday	Tuesday	Wednesday	Thursday	Friday
9.00	Break area	Break area	Break area	Break area	Break area
9.20	Work with teacher	Work with teacher	Work with teacher	Work with teacher	Work with teacher
9.40	Greeting and news Singing	Greeting and news Singing	Greeting and news Singing	Greeting and news Singing	Greeting and news Singing
10.00	Independent work	Independent work	Independent work	Independent work	Independent work
10.30	Computer	Computer	Computer	Computer	Computer
10.45	Break area	Break area	Break area	Break area	Break area
11.00	Outdoor play	Outdoor play	Outdoor play	Outdoor play	Outdoor play
11.10	Board games: Language	Interactive play	Board games: Number	Sensory play: Play-Doh	Sensory play: Sand
11.30	Structured play	Structured play	Structured play	Structured play	Structured play
12.00	Group work	Group work	Group work	Group work	Group work
12.15	Exercises	Exercises	Exercises	Exercises	Exercises
12.30	Lunch	Lunch	Lunch	Lunch	Lunch

12.45	Outdoor play	Outdoor play	Outdoor play	Outdoor play	Outdoor play
1.00	Independent work	Independent work	Independent work	Independent work	Independent work
1.30	P.E.	Library	Music	Art and craft	P.E.
2.00	Work with teacher	Work with teacher	Work with teacher	Work with teacher	Work with teacher
2.30	Break area	Break area	Break area	Break area	Break area
2.40	Reflection	Reflection	Reflection	Reflection	Reflection
3.00	Home	Home	Home	Home	Home

Figure 5.5 shows an 'Independent Work' schedule-slip that as the teacher I would complete with a child during our one-to-one session earlier in a day or the day before the work was required. While it visually reminded the child of the work s/he had to do, it also encouraged and developed reading, comprehension and independence skills.

Work To Do

Order	Work	Finished
1.		
2.		
3.		

Figure 5.5 An example of an 'Independent Work' schedule-slip.
To be completed by the teacher with a child during their one-to-one work session in preparation for independent work later that day or on the following day.

I would write detailed instructions on the schedule-slip. These instructions could include the subject, name of textbook, page and exercise they had to complete. The calm, confidence and competency with which children who were working with these schedule-slips set about and accomplished their daily tasks was a joy to observe. They all, without exception, appeared focused, incredibly mature and remarkably amazing!

Nevertheless, it is important to reiterate that while the visual timetables referred to are developmental in nature, there should be absolutely no expectation that any individual child will or should progress through some or all of the stages. The value, purpose and goals of visual aids/schedules lie in a child's learning of ownership, understanding and de-stressing rather than any upward progression, regardless of how welcome that may be.

Also, there are three elements in formulating a visual schedule that require consideration. The first is directionality. I strongly recommend that visual timetables are horizontal until the child has developed a dominant left–right orientation. The horizontal directionality of their daily schedule/s will assist in the development of this orientation. It is important to note that, as with many early years children, young children with autism often have a right–left orientation. In other words, they are inclined to view, draw, scribble or work from right to left rather than the left-to-right directionality of European languages. This is most clearly identified when a young child starts to form individual letters. For example, a lower case 'b' formed using a right-to-left orientation will start with the round bottom curve moving to a bottom-up stroke for the back. This orientation, whilst manageable at a print stage of handwriting, is known to cause difficulties at a joined-up or cursive stage of handwriting. Therefore, some in the field of handwriting teaching advocate the abandonment of the print-to-joined-up letters approach traditionally applied in British and Irish schools. Their contemporary approach holds that as soon as a child knows how to orientate and form letters properly with 'tails' for joining them, they should be taught joined handwriting, and isolated letters should only be revisited when there is a clear need to.[1]

The second element to consider is the cognitive development of the child. Usually with children under three years of age it is necessary to introduce a visual timetable with objects and separate but accompanying words. Single words may be used, such as write, puzzle or lunch. However, some teachers may prefer to amalgamate exposure to the written word with an introduction to representational pictures, as in Figure 5.6.

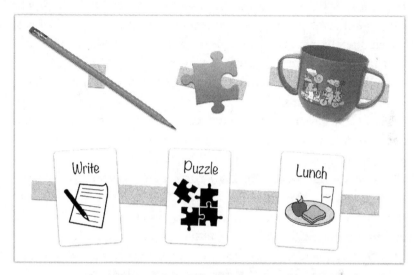

Figure 5.6 An example of a timetable.
This amalgamates 'objects of reference' with representational pictures and the written word for a young child starting school.

However, there are some under-threes with autism who are word aware, having understood the relationship between a spoken and written word through cognitive ability enabled by familial input and/or environmental influences. When faced with a child with this ability, the danger for some carers is to assume that comprehension is intrinsic to word recognition, and to remove the concrete visual aid of an object, photograph, picture or icon too soon. This can be a serious mistake because there are children with autism who develop the ability to read without an equivalent development in their comprehension.

The condition known as 'hyperlexia' describes a very young child with what is termed a 'precocious' reading ability. Hyperlexia is not unique to children with autism. There are neurotypical children whose early reading prowess is impressive, but usually their peers catch them up, and they do not exhibit a significant discrepancy between their reading and comprehension age. The same is sadly not always true for children with autism. Although some professionals have argued that children with autism can fall into one or two categories of hyperlexia, separating children without comprehension difficulties from those with, as the diagnosis of autism includes difficulties with language there is normally some comprehension need even if this is merely literal inference or interpretative. Also, advocates of this view usually raise the issue of savants. However, the global statistics for savants does not augur well for a large group with autism but without comprehension needs.

Savant syndrome is not only extremely rare but also does not describe across-the-board extraordinary abilities.[2] Savant syndrome describes what is popularly termed 'islands' or 'islets' of extraordinary ability. Also, statistically only 50 per cent of savants are believed to have autism. The other 50 per cent have developmental delays, learning disabilities and central nervous system (CNS) injuries. For example, Saloviita, Ruusila and Ruusila (2000), in a study of no less than 583 residential facilities for persons with learning disabilities, found a prevalence rate of 1.4 savants per every 1000 residents.

Statistics regarding how many persons with autism are savants also vary from 1 in every 10 (Rimland 1978) to as low as Hermelin's (2001) more recent conjecture of 1 in every 200. In other words, using recent UK statistics in which 1 in every 100 people is believed to have autism, Rimland's (1978) statistical conjecture estimates that 0.1 per cent of the population will have both autism and savant syndrome while Hermelin's (2001) figures suggest a much lower percentage of 0.005 per cent! Meanwhile, in the USA, where the statistics shorten to 1 in every 68 people with autism, using Rimland's (1978) statistics, 0.15 per cent approximately will have both conditions but with Hermelin's (2001) figures drops to 0.0074 per cent. Not very strong statistics in any scenario.

Finally, as savant syndrome describes 'islands' or 'islets' of genius, there is the question of whether the skill of reading and the ability to comprehend the spoken or written word are all one and the same island.

So to the actual timetables/schedules themselves. Table 5.2 is a brief synopsis of visual mediums and design orientations as children move from early years/profound need to secondary school work.

Table 5.2 Possible progressive visual mediums and orientations as children move from early years/ profound need to secondary school work.

Development	Visual mediums	Design orientation
First/Then	Objects of reference with separate words	Horizontal
First/Next/Last	Objects of reference with separate words or photographs with separate words	Horizontal
First/Next/Then/Last	Objects of reference with separate words, photographs with separate words or pictures with words	Horizontal
Schedules demarcating the day, e.g. from arrival to first play, from end of first play to lunch and from end of lunch to home time	Photographs with separate words or pictures with words or icons with words (Some objects of reference may still be in use at this stage)	Horizontal
Schedules dividing the day into morning and afternoon sessions	Icons with words or words only (Some pictures with words may still be in use at this stage)	Horizontal
A whole day schedule	Words only	Once a child shows competence at the whole word stage the orientation can change to the vertical

Introduced even at a pre-school age, these timetables enable independence and reduce stress.

Finally, as with the stress-reducing strategies/practices listed in 'De-Stress Strategies/Practices' above, children with autism should be visually aided to know, understand and conform to a school's behavioural code. Classroom codes of behaviour/school rules should be displayed in simple, clear language with accompanying pictures if appropriate. These should be few and consistent throughout the school and with long-term relevance to the social world. Also, as much as possible, they should take a positive rather than negative approach to conduct, for example 'Walk inside the school building' instead of 'Do not run inside the school building'. It is also important to remember when writing these rules and/or codes of behaviour that children with autism may interpret them literally and rigidly, so it is advisable not to set in stone any rule or code of behaviour that may need to be changed later.

Ultimately, the combined importance of the stress-reducing strategies and all forms of visual aids cannot be overestimated in a school fit for all children because, whilst there may not be a child with autism in every classroom, there will be more than one or two visual learners.[3]

Consider Sensory Needs

As Chapter 7 details some sensory considerations necessary for children with autism, I will not develop these ideas here. It is sufficient to note that the sensory needs of a child with autism should be given significant considerations in all individualised educational planning.

Countdown Transitions

It is well recognised that times of transition/change are some of the most stressful for children with autism, and stress for a child with autism can frequently translate into challenging behaviours. Sometimes adults, wishing to avoid these distressing situations, spring a change upon a child, hoping that the suddenness will circumvent difficulties. Yes, there may be a moment of pause underpinned by confusion, but I have rarely seen this 'surprise' strategy work successfully.

Preparation for a child with autism is usually the key to a less stressful and manageable transition. As with the time awareness adults grant to their own transitions, checking the time and invariably allowing themselves to complete some aspect of a task before moving onto another task or place, a child with autism should be prepared for a move from one activity/place to the next, especially when the current activity is a preferred one but the next is not. The countdown can be given verbally or visually – ideally, in the early stages, both. The countdown with which I had the best results starts at 5 minutes reducing to 1 minute, and then to a 10, 9, 8, 7, 6, 5, 4, 3, 2, 1 final countdown.

Usually a young child, even with autism, has no real-time frame for one minute, making the countdown minutes as flexible as the adult needs. However, some children with autism can develop a strong sense of time as they mature, so supplementing sand-timers and/or timers for the manual countdown becomes a necessity.

Be Honest and Straightforward

One of the most important practices for those working and/or living with children with autism is to avoid making requests where there is no choice. The social nuances of asking a child to do something that is required may be lost on a child with autism. By requesting rather than requiring, the adult has implied choice where there is none, that is, there is usually something you want the child to do, such as change an activity, move to another position, put shoes/clothes on, do homework and so forth. Moreover, as a direct consequence of this inaccuracy, I have many times witnessed the adult unintentionally create a challenging situation in which s/he requires a child to perform some task, but the misleading, implied choice has liberated the child from the necessity of doing what was asked. Hence, do not give choice where there is none. If you want a child with autism to do something, do not use polite phrases such as 'I would like you to...' or 'Would you...?' Instead, take personal responsibility for what you want the child to do, prefacing the requirement with 'I want you...' In this way, there is no misunderstanding, while, as a by-product, honesty and personal responsibility are modelled.

Also, avoid threats of any sort. These include the threat of another adult, such as 'the lady' or 'man' in a shop or 'the head/principal' in a school. Again, having issued a threat, if the child chooses to ignore or reject it, a challenging situation can ensue. Hence, it is far better for all concerned for the adult to once again take personal responsibility for the action they wish a child to do by clearly stating, 'I want you to come to the table/do your homework/put away your jigsaw puzzle', and so on.

Alternatively, whenever possible, do give a choice to a child with autism, offering 'this' or 'that'. Choice is important for children with rigid and routine interests or occupations. Additionally, observing the choices a child with autism makes is a highly informative source of insight for parents and professionals wishing to know what motivates a child. In fact, it is a method used by some autism-specific approaches, such as PECS, to compile a list of motivators and to preferentially order them.

Be Proactive

This guideline follows in the spirit of the previous one in its advice to avoid threats of any kind. Threats usually arise reactively to situations and circumstances adults wish to overcome or change. They come in many different forms. There are overt threats of punishment, such as 'If you don't do...I will take away your football/computer/mobile phone.' Then there are more covert and manipulative threats, such as 'If you don't go to bed now Father Christmas won't come!' or 'The lady is going to come over and shout at you!' The problem with a threat, especially for a child with autism, is that once issued, if ignored by the child, it must be carried out by the adult. So the football, computer or mobile phone must be removed, Father Christmas cannot come and the lady must come over and shout at the miscreant child. If the threatened scenario does not occur, rigidity of thinking swiftly transforms into adult impotency. In other words, the child quickly learns and comprehends that there are no real threats.

Threats are not only generally reactive but they also tend to corner the child. They do so because they usually contain an intrinsic, simplified equation: if you do this or you don't do this, this will happen or follow. In other words, they corner a child by offering no other way through an impasse than compliance with one required behaviour or action. Furthermore, it was my experience that when adults 'corner' a child they have generally placed themselves in the corner too! Offering a child a simplified one-solution threat removes the adult's ability to negotiate, too. This creates a power struggle in which the adult may perceive a loss of control that may emotionally raise the ante and tip an already precarious situation.

Therefore, proactive measures are always preferable to reactive ones because they foresee areas of difficulty and seek to avoid them before they happen. However, for parents and professionals alike, putting into place proactive measures can be challenging. Reactive practices can take hold unconsciously and swiftly, while proactive ones always take time, reflection and adjustment to formulate and become effective. Also, as reactive practices take hold, parents usually feel physically and emotionally drained, while their frontline counterparts in schools experience the heavy weight of personal responsibility and inadequacy. These leave all parties exhausted, overwhelmed, vulnerable and in no fit state to implement the necessary changes.

Thus, proactive measures may require a high level of co-operation, collaboration and compassion to muster the necessary strength needed for formulation and consistent, persevering implementation. Effective planning and implementation may require shared knowledge of the child, a united intervention plan and mutual respect based upon goodwill between all concerned parties. For example, the scenario of the overt threat 'If you don't do your homework/school work I will take away your football' is avoided by the introduction of a visual schedule in which the child is made aware that, at home and at school, work sessions are followed by brief sessions in which the child is given a football to kick around. In this scenario the football has become a positive 'reinforcer' rather than a negative punishment.

Finally, if there is a consistent proactive approach across the familial, leisure and educational environments a child frequents, effectiveness can eventually be judged by the child and the adult stepping out of the dark corners of challenging interactions and behaviours and into the new realm of choice and negotiation. For example, the child may choose to have a computer session after a homework/school work session instead of kicking a football around.

Praise

Praise is an essential part of a proactive approach. Threats focus on negative, unwelcome behaviours and consequences, but praise focuses on the positive behaviours adults wish to encourage.

However, with both praise and threat the language adults predominantly use can construct either a 'good' or a 'naughty' child. Both are emotionally charged and are best avoided. Personally, I have always worked with the premise that there are no innately good or bad children; there are just behaviours that are positive and appropriate and behaviours that are best described as challenging. So, as threat is reactive and to be avoided, in this section I will focus on praise as a proactive intervention of choice. In doing so I hope to show how it can be used to name and reinforce appropriate, positive behaviours.

When praising a child with autism, focus on the behaviour you wish recognised and reinforced. For example, 'Good writing!', 'Good listening!' and 'Good eating!' This terminology names an appropriate behaviour and acknowledges it. It also gives a child attention for positive behaviour, and as a welcome bonus it can develop a child's knowledge of verbs.

The best news regarding this approach is that it tends to exponentially increase, gathering momentum with use. Also, used frequently this is an approach that has the power to break destructive, downward spiralling relationships as adults start to focus on the appropriate behaviours of the child rather than the challenging ones that may have overwhelmed them. Thus, the art of praising a child with autism is a powerful means of revitalising exhausted, overwhelmed and vulnerable parents and professionals, and transforming negative, downward spiralling relationship cycles into positive, manageable ones.

Foster Independence

In my opinion, the most underestimated characteristic of autism is 'rigidity of thinking'. During my practice I observed many children rapidly develop routines and behavioural sequences that they and others had to adhere to, and I concluded that 'rigidity of thinking' is the predominant force behind most challenging behaviours. These could spring from a singular event in which the auto-centred nature of autism had been satisfied, and then the rigidity of thinking had solidified it into an imperative. For example, when learning to sit at a table with others, a hungry child with autism may display impatience and frustration that is inadvertently rewarded by being served first. Next, the combination of auto-centred satisfaction, rewarded behaviour and fixation on sameness may exacerbate challenging behaviours because the child now expects to be served first. The more this is repeated, the greater the behaviours are reinforced and set fast.

When this insight is applied to schoolwork, the importance of encouraging independent work from the earliest school days can be thoroughly understood. From the start of school, the aim should be the development of sound, independent working skills. Therefore, while there is a time and a place for a teacher or instructor to work one-to-one, sitting next to or by a child, when undertaking a task that requires independent working, adults should not sit with or in any way engage the child's attention. Instead facilitation or prompting should be used. Facilitation and prompting includes:

- pointing to the next part of the work

- physical facilitation that reduces and extinguishes as quickly as possible, such as an adult's hand guiding a child's hand, reducing to an adult's hand guiding from the wrist and then to the elbow until there is no need for guidance

- verbally saying 'Next'

- pointing at visual schedules and/or verbally reminding the child what s/he is working for, for example pointing to the object/picture/word 'computer' which is the next activity on the schedule

- applying deep pressure on the child's shoulders.

Given the hustle and bustle of many classrooms, fostering independent work for a child with autism often requires the considered provision of a quiet place to work. In the TEACCH approach this is called a 'workstation'. A workstation comprises a child's desk that is positioned to minimise distraction while enabling good, independent work practices. This often implies having the desk facing a blank wall free from visual stimulants such as posters and pictures. I found it practical and useful to have the individual child's schedule displayed at working eye level, and to equip the workstation with some writing and working tools/aids, such as pencils, rulers and number lines or squares. Also, as I could give each child their own workstation, their independent work was presented in filing trays or an inbox on the left-hand side. The completed work task could then be placed into filing trays or an outbox on the right-hand side.

At workstations, as indicated by placing 'to do' work on the left-hand side and finished work on the right-hand side, I strongly recommend that the flow of work follows the directionality of the reading/writing system the child is being introduced to. Also, to enable independence, children should have access to a visual schedule. If it is not possible to give each child their own individual workstation it may be necessary, as in many TEACCH classrooms, to display these at a central desk. Alternatively, in a mainstream classroom it may be easier to have a large, whole class schedule displayed at some vantage point within the room. Clearly these are issues pertinent to the individual teacher, child and class.

At home, fostering independence is equally necessary. To avoid the combination of 'auto' and 'rigidity of thinking' creating challenging behaviours and habits, it is important to encourage independence in all areas of the child's life from as early as possible. Rigid habits and challenging behaviours are more difficult to extinguish than to prevent. Hence, making allowances for a child because of his/her autism is one of the biggest mistakes parents and extended family can make.

At home, children with autism should be encouraged, from the earliest consideration that they may be on the spectrum, to dress, toilet, eat, work and sleep independently. Homework is another issue best addressed as early as possible to achieve the necessary routine and independence. Hence, creating a workstation at home for a child bringing school work home for the first time can prove a highly pre-emptive measure.

Furthermore, especially in the early stages when homework is being introduced, it is advisable for it to be regular and easy. Regularity and ease enable young children to readily adopt the process. For example, with early years students I would send work home on Monday afternoons and collect it in on Friday mornings, enabling families adjusting to the home–school routines to develop a familial schedule that suited the whole family best. The ease of the work sent home is important, too. Especially in the early years, making assignments easy can reduce stress levels for a whole family. Homework should provide an opportunity for the parent/s or carer/s of young children to actively share in their child's learning. It should not bring more stress into a home or add more weight onto possibly already pressurised home-time. Before and beyond homework, young children with autism need to play games, undertake social activities, learn life skills and have fun with their parents and siblings. Therefore I strongly recommend that, for children with autism who are experiencing the first few years of school, the focus of homework should not be upon the work to be completed, but rather on the following:

- The establishment of good homework routines for the child that will make family life easier in the long term.

- The development of good hand–motor skills, letter orientation and directionality, because in my experience children with autism often have 'handwriting' difficulties. Thus, in the early stages it is very important that, with as stress-free endeavours as possible, they are encouraged to hold their pencil/crayon with the correct tripod grip, that is, thumb and first finger pinched on either side of the pencil, and supported underneath by the second/middle finger. Also, it is equally important that, with as little stress as possible to those assisting them, they are encouraged to form letters correctly, that is, a top-down, anti-clockwise orientation with letters being formed in one continuous stroke.[4]

- A chance for parents/carers to reinforce book awareness, such as the directionality of text. Also, an opportunity to gain an insight into their child's aptitude and attitude to do independent 'book' learning. Whilst homework is now seen as an established time for parents/carers to share in their children's education, for children with autism it is also the perfect opportunity in which to gradually and occasionally withdraw both assistance and attention to establish independent working skills as early as possible. When doing so, the facilitation and prompting strategies previously outlined are very useful. Applying them will also ensure a degree of consistency between school and home.

- Finally, early years homework can also provide the opportunity to encourage and teach children how to pursue interests and gain insight and information. This includes visits to places of local interest, libraries, museums and galleries, and looking things up on the web.

Teach Change

Overall, for children with autism, rigidity of thinking leads to repetitious behaviours, preoccupations with routines and patterns, and the need for 'sameness'. In a confusing, complex universe, order and control is maintained through familiarity and sameness. Familiarity and sameness enable predictable events and outcomes. Predictable events and outcomes are stress-free experiences. Thus a child with autism in a comforting, routine manner, day after day, will eat the same food, drink the same drink, make the same jigsaw puzzle, draw the same cartoon, arrange the same pattern/sequence and so on endlessly.

In my opinion there is nothing innately amiss with this. All human beings are de-stressed and comforted by daily routines and habits. However, accidentally breaking routines and habits does not cause the neurotypical mind quite the same stress and distress that is usually observed when a child with autism has a precious ritual disturbed or denied. Generally, a neurotypical child will enjoy the adventure of discovering a new interest/occupation, of learning a different way to perform/do something or to travel to a familiar place. However, with children with autism it is more common to observe rising anxiety with change, unpredictability and 'newness'. Furthermore, this rising anxiety can be expressed as challenging behaviours, such as self-harm. Therefore, from an early age it is in the best interests of children with autism to extend and to teach them change.

There are many ways in which change can be taught. These include simple considerations, such as taking different routes to a frequent destination, varying food and shopping in different locations. They also include planned interventions, particularly those that widen leisure/pleasure activities.

Extending and developing leisure activities should be an essential part of the educational experience of children with autism. In a classroom this can be accomplished by having a small area dedicated to this purpose and equipped with activities that are predominantly table-top activities with a leisure or play basis, such as puzzles, peg boards, figures to dress and undress, and construction models to make and/or complete. All that this area requires is a shelving unit that enables activities to be clearly and independently displayed and labelled for students to independently access and tidy away and a table/desk to complete them on.[5]

Also, these leisure activities should usually stem from a pre-existing interest of the child that is being either extended or developed. The extension and/or development must be introduced to the child in a one-to-one situation with an adult and the child must have acquired a degree of independent competency in completing the activity before the activity is placed on the display shelves for him/her to access at the scheduled time.

Importantly, all activities must have a clear starting and finishing point enabling children to recognise where to start and finish activities before replacing them on the appropriate shelf.

Clearly extending and teaching change, whether a simple consideration or a planned intervention, requires individualised forward planning. For example, as with the provision of structured play activities that requires knowledge of the child's interests and abilities, varying routes taken from home to familiar destinations is also best supported by some forethought and planning. In such an instance, varying journeys could be supported by simple, child-friendly maps drawn by a parent/carer. Following and matching illustrated maps to the actual routes taken may occupy the child's mind, reducing or extinguishing anxiety. It would also encourage the development of cognitive skills and abilities.

Mission Statement for a School Fit to Serve Children with Autism

In conclusion, I offer a draft of a mission statement for any school that aspires to welcome and appropriately accommodate our different thinkers:

- We aim to enable each individual student to develop academically and socially to their fullest, independent potential.

- We promise to endeavour never to forget the individuality and diversity of our students, constantly seeking to know and address their educational needs, acknowledge their individual strengths, respect their differences and celebrate all learning and progress no matter how small or incremental it may appear.

- To do so we ask that those with whom we work encourage and enable us to vigilantly and positively self-reflect, questioning our own preconceptions least we become rigid, unrealistic and limited in our demands and vision of/for our students, others in our teams and ultimately ourselves.

- We believe that the success of this work is dependent on communication, co-operation and collaboration between staff, students, parents and external professionals. To achieve this, we acknowledge the need for all to share responsibilities, support decisions agreed upon and avoid conflict or blame.

- Ultimately we aspire to create a safe, calm, warm and friendly environment conducive to the learning of all our students and the well-being of all who work and learn within our school.

Notes

1. Additionally, some professionals in the field of specific learning difficulties such as dyslexia have long argued that teaching joined handwriting is an aid to spelling.
2. Savant syndrome is not presently medically recognised or listed.
3. Be mindful of visual and kinaesthetic processing needs: As an addendum to the use of visual aids, a school fit to serve all, including children with autism, would recognise the differing needs of different learning styles. In the case of children with autism and visual learners, it would anticipate the need for increased preparation and practice time for unfamiliar events. Also, these rehearsals which could be phased in or out to

suit individual needs and strengths would have heightened visual and kinaesthetic elements.

4. Many schools today adopt a cursive/joined script from infants upwards. This is an approach strongly recommended for children with dyslexia. As it helps children with a specific learning difficulty, it makes sense that it can help most children. However, it does mean that, whilst promoting top-down directionality, the child starts to form the letter from the line with a bottom-up hand movement, which can initially be confusing for any child.

5. Some younger children and/or children with high levels of emotional-behavioural needs may require their structured play area being incorporated into their workstation to reduce movement and/or distress.

Chapter 6

BEHAVIOUR MANAGEMENT

Introduction

This chapter examines the reasons why children with autism may have greater propensity to challenging behaviours than their neurotypical peers. In doing so I present the arguments that rigidity of thinking may be the predominant cause and that these behaviours are in themselves communicative. These ideas are based upon my own experiences as a teacher of children with autism.

Also, from the baseline that rigidity of thinking underpins challenging behaviours, and that these behaviours have a communicative role, I explore how crises can be prevented and managed. This includes looking at change and transition, which are extremely challenging for children with autism. It also includes suggestions for making school trips stress-free, enjoyable events for children and adults alike, and classrooms more autism and visual learner-friendly places.

Autism and Challenging Behaviours

Children with autism have a higher propensity to develop challenging behaviours than their neurotypical peers. The reason for this is commonly attributed to sensory issues and/or miscomprehended social codes and rules. However, in my practice I came to believe that the predominant reason lies in the rigidity of thinking that accompanies autism. Moreover, I came to identify three distinct ways in which this often underpins challenging behaviours.

The first way I have touched upon in the previous chapter in the section entitled 'Foster Independence'. It is when routines and ritualistic behaviours, satisfying an auto-centred desire, are disturbed, threatened or changed, provoking anxiety-driven challenging behaviours.

The second way is when challenging behaviours are themselves manifestations of rigidity of thinking, as in learned behaviours. For example, in the scenario of a child who must be the first in all events, the learned behaviour of a high-pitched scream may ensue if this required order is threatened or overturned. Suppose the first time someone went to give food/drink to another child before the child with autism, the child with autism responded with a high-pitched scream. This screaming may have momentarily immobilised the adult but eventually s/he may have turned to the child with autism and to stop her/him screaming given him/her what was wanted. Clearly, it can be seen from this scenario how satisfying the auto-centred demand to be first leads to the formulation of the challenging behaviour of high-pitched screaming. Every time the situation was repeated, if the behaviour was reinforced with further immediate satisfaction a learned behaviour would emerge. Unfortunately, once an inappropriate or challenging behaviour is habitually established, it can take great time and patience to extinguish.

The third way in which rigid thinking can lead to challenging behaviours relates to what I describe as 'core constructs'. I was only able to explore this pathway with children with mild autism, or what was then known as Asperger's syndrome (AS), because of the language-weighted interactions required to investigate individual 'core constructs'. My inquiries were based on the premise that for many children with autism reality can be singular: what they constitute as reality is the only reality, common and known to all. Given that premise, how a child responds to events and situations is governed by the child's singular viewpoint that s/he presumes is shared by others. Thus, I encountered children with AS who did not understand or appreciate the need to explain their behaviours to responsible adults because they believed that they already knew and understood the situation from their singular, shared viewpoint. In other words, there were no multiple perspectives, just one – theirs. For example, a young man with mild autism attacked his own team's goalkeeper during a football match. For many hours after the match he silently and angrily refused to explain his actions. To some degree his silence and anger emanated from his belief that I already knew his explanation; how could I not when there was only a singular version of reality! However, there was another side to his silent, angry behaviour. It was his deeply held 'core construct' of justice and his right to 'pay back' wrongdoers. Eventually he explained to me that the job of a goalkeeper was to stop goals being scored against his team. It turned out that the goalkeeper he attacked had let in a home goal. The young man's 'core construct' of justice and his right to 'pay back' wrongdoers allowed for this errant goalkeeper to be punished. Only when I understood this 'core construct' could I begin to deal appropriately with his challenging behaviours.

'Core constructs', as the name implies, are deeply rooted within an individual's sense of self and identity, and as with roots of great trees their grip can be extremely enduring and deep. Hence it was my experience that trying to eliminate a 'core construct' was not the way to approach behavioural management. Besides, for me a root construct of justice is an innately positive 'core construct' for anyone to have. For example, in the case of the young man who attacked his team's goalkeeper, it was the root to other positive behaviours, such as befriending and defending younger children who he saw as being 'picked on' by others.

Alternatively, I concluded that challenging behaviours that arise from rigidly held 'core constructs' are best managed by the explicit teaching of social rules and codes of behaviour. Designed to keep challenging behaviours in check, these individualised social rules and codes act as lids, containing behaviours at a higher awareness level than the deep, subconscious strata of the personal constructs. To obtain this higher awareness level they need to be simple, visual, targeted and reinforced. Figures 6.1, 6.2, 6.3 and 6.4 are four examples of social rules and codes of behaviour.

The Anger Rules

It is **OK** to feel angry
BUT

X **DON'T** hurt others
X **DON'T** hurt yourself
X **DON'T** hurt property

* **DO** TALK ABOUT IT *

Figure 6.1 Example 1 of a visual social rule/code of behaviour.
Using colour with such visual aids is helpful. For example, in this case the title
and crosses would be best in red and the asterisks and word 'DO' in green.

Winning & Losing!

These are the possible outcomes of arguments, disagreements or fights.
Only the last one lets both sides walk away happily.

1. One Winner & One Loser
With this outcome, the winner is happy but the loser is unhappy.
So, the unhappy loser may want revenge and do
something bad to the winner. Best AVOID this outcome!

2. A Draw
With a draw, someone may still feel the need to have another go at winning.
It is like a football match. The teams may need to play again.
Best to be aware of this!

3. Both Winners
When both sides walk away feeling they have won something, both sides are happy.
Feeling you have won something may be feeling heard, being given an apology,
being given a promise that it will not
happen again or even being given time with something you wanted.
ALWAYS GO after this outcome and you will have a great life!

Figure 6.2 Example 2 of a visual social rule/code of behaviour.
Again the use of colour would increase the effectiveness of this image. For
example, point 1 would be best in red, point 2 in orange/yellow and point 3 in
green, reflecting the colours for stop/prepare/go in the traffic light sequence.

The Domino Effect!

Every argument
Every fight
Every act of aggression
Starts
With one domino falling.
The rest just follows on.

The first domino is the first inappropriate act.

Accidentally knocking a pencil off a desk is not inappropriate.

Disagreeing about the answer is not inappropriate.

Responding offensively is inappropriate.
Kicking, name calling, tripping, hitting and shoving are all inappropriate.

REMEMBER
If the first domino does not happen/fall, the other dominoes will remain standing!

Figure 6.3 Example 3 of a visual social rule/code of behaviour.[1]

Spectrum of Competitiveness

Good Loser - **Bad Loser**

REMEMBER
Most people learn to be in the middle somewhere.
BUT most people would rather win than lose.

No one can see how we are feeling but everyone can see how we act.
Feelings are invisible but actions are visible.

Good losers may feel disappointed
but they **bravely** congratulate
the winner.

Figure 6.4 Example 4 of a visual social rule/code of behaviour.
Again the use of colour would increase the effectiveness of this image. For
example, the words 'Good Loser' would be best in green and 'Bad Loser'
in red; the dotted line between the words 'Good Loser' and 'Bad Loser'
could be coloured green for the third nearest 'Good Loser', orange/yellow
for the third in the middle, and red for the third nearest 'Bad Loser'.

Challenging Behaviours as Communication

Clearly then, challenging behaviours are frequently communicating needs, desires and 'core construct' drives. When these behaviours are understood as communicative, it is not surprising that children with autism, who often struggle with the expression of needs and wants, should have a greater propensity to develop them than their peers. Unable to adequately express their desires, they can be overwhelmed by strong emotions, such as anger and frustration: the emotions often seen in a meltdown.

A forked intervention approach is needed. First, the child with autism who is experiencing the difficulty should be helped to understand and appropriately express their emotions. Second, attending adults need to find ways to make their own communication more readily understood through methods that make it simpler, that is, more exact and graphic.

Both strands of this forked intervention may include the use of visual aids and the devising of explicit social rules and codes of behaviour, as shown in Figures 6.1, 6.2, 6.3 and 6.4. Currently there are three popular methods that embrace these features. They are the following.

Social Stories™

The concept of 'Social Stories™' was created by Carol Gray in the 1990s. Social Stories™ are brief scenarios describing specific situations, events or activities pertinent to a child's life, for example a trip to the dentist, having nails cut or how to brush teeth. They include the significant information about what to expect and to do in a situation and explain why concisely and precisely. They can also contain individual-appropriate positive, reassuring phrases, such as 'It will be good!' or 'I will try!'

Social Stories™ further emotional understanding and appropriate expression. They also foster behavioural strategies and enable adults to make their own communication more readily understood. They target and develop self-care skills, such as washing hands, cleaning teeth, using the toilet appropriately and dressing/undressing; and self-management and social skills, such as turn-taking and waiting.

Ultimately, they enable understanding of a behaviour and the responses of others in social situations. Additionally they can help a child through routine changes and unexpected or distressing events, such as starting school, changing classrooms and moving home.

In her book *The New Social Story Book* (1994a), Gray outlined guidelines on the effective use of Social Stories™. These were:

- Introduce one story at a time to focus and maximise learning without overwhelming and/or confusing the child.

- Present the story to the child when you are both relaxed and calm, thereby maximising the learning potential and enabling positive associations with the story and content. Gray (1994a) stipulated that Social Stories™ should never be used as a punishment for inappropriate or challenging behaviours.

- Be honest and straightforward when introducing a story. For example, 'I have written a story for you about why children in school put their hands up to ask and answer questions. We are going to read it together now.'

- Read the story with the child as often as is required. For example, a Social Story™ about visiting the dentist may be read frequently in advance of a planned visit.

- When reading a story with a child, the adult should remain positive, reassuring and patient, and this should be reflected in a calm and friendly tone of voice.

- The surroundings in which the story is read should be quiet, comfortable and distraction free.

- When appropriate, involve others in the reading of the story. For example, a Social Story™ regarding a school-based situation can be read at home with parents and other carers, as well as in school with the teacher and support staff.

- 'Fade' a story out instead of simply abandoning it. Gray (1994a) recommended two ways of fading. The first was to increase the time between readings, for example if a story was being read twice a day, this could be reduced to once, then to every other day and so on. The second method was to change the content of the story so that it reflected the child's new skills/ knowledge, for example directive sentences can be removed, replaced by statements, or even partially rewritten, requiring the child to recall and verbalise the missing information. However, regarding the second method, Gray (1994a) acknowledged that for some children with autism changes to a well-loved story can be very distressing and, if this is the case, alternative means of 'fading' are necessary.

Comic Strips

Carol Gray (1994b) also created Comic Strip Conversations. These are simple cartoon-like representations of thought-bubble conversations that can show how people may be feeling, their intentions and what they said. In so doing, as with Social Stories™, they can assist emotional understanding, appropriate expression and effective behavioural strategies whilst enabling adults to make their own communication more readily and graphically understood.

Comic Strip Conversations combine talk with drawing, and use stick figures, drawings, symbols and colour to present visually different elements and nuances of a conversation. For example, colours may be used to indicate the different feelings of people in a situation. Therefore, some of the more abstract components/concepts of social communication and interaction are made more concrete and understandable; and the perspectives of others are made known.

To create a Comic Strip Conversation, the child with autism takes the lead role, but the parent, carer or professional initiates the exchange and provides the necessary insight and guidance throughout the process. For example, a teacher may initiate a conversation about the contents of a child's lunchbox, encouraging the child to draw the contents being discussed. As this familiarises the child with combining talking with drawing, it is also mimicking everyday social conversations. Next the teacher may ask several questions regarding a specific event, situation or social interaction, guiding the child with autism to verbalise and draw their responses. Sometimes complex situations require a sequence of comic strip boxes that should be numbered to reflect their place in the sequence of events. Then, before the comic strip conversation is concluded, the attending adult should revisit the discussion, summarising the event or situation using the child's drawings. From this interaction the adult can seek to address any problems or concerns that have been identified, and thereby develop action plans for the child with autism to recall and implement in similar future situations.

Additionally, Comic Strip Conversations can be used to plan for unfamiliar future situations that a child with autism identifies as inducing anxiety or concern. However, as situations and circumstances can change prior to an event, the information relating to the future must allow for the unexpected.

Diagrams/Charts

Diagrams, charts and maps can present information that assists emotional understanding, appropriate expression and effective behavioural strategies whilst enabling adults to make their own communications more readily and graphically understood. As children with autism often experience language and attention challenges that make learning from verbal explanations difficult, visual diagrams, charts and so on can make concepts more concretely understandable. Also, the logical, often sequential flow of information presented in these forms can more powerfully engage the attention of children with autism than verbalisations and, unlike the spoken word, they can revisit these pictorial aids as often as necessary.

In terms of assisting emotional understanding, appropriate expression and effective behavioural strategies whilst enabling adults to make their own communications more readily and graphically understood, Figure 6.5 shows how the consequences for making either the appropriate or the inappropriate choice can be explained to a young child with autism.

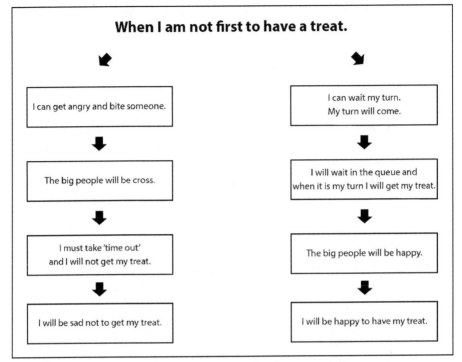

Figure 6.5 How the consequences of making/taking an inappropriate choice or action can be visually presented and explained.
Traffic light colours should be used with orange/yellow for the top statement, red for the inappropriate response column and green for the appropriate response column.

Challenging Behaviours and Crisis

When 'rigidity of thinking' is understood as the predominant root of challenging behaviours, the habitual nature and the ease and dangers of reinforcing them becomes immensely clear. The method of responding is also made evident.

First, I believe it is important to include a description of this method, because to dismiss, ignore or play down the issue of challenging behaviours in relation to autism is akin to leaving carers exposed to extreme elements without any form of protection. Therefore the measures presented encompass the worst case scenario of physically threatening behaviour, although they are applicable to many challenging situations.

Second, I believe that awareness usually leads to proactive rather than reactive approaches, with which challenging behaviours are at least minimalised and at best avoided altogether. In my experience avoiding the onset of a challenging behaviour has been easier and swifter in implementation than extinguishing one.

Finally, over-arching all measures and approaches, it is important not to assume or assign blame to a child, oneself or others. For me, we are dealing with communication in the form of an emerging skill borne from how the brain with autism works rather than conscious, deliberate intent. Unfortunately, communication in the form of a challenging behaviour is not a skill we wish to encourage or reinforce. Certainly, the behaviour being witnessed may have been negatively reinforced in the past, but the focus must now be on extinguishing it rather than assigning blame.

Outside Crisis

When it is known that a child may present with challenging behaviours there should be a three-stage planned approach in place. The first stage relates to what needs to be known and in place prior to a challenging behaviour crisis. The second relates to what needs to be known and focused on during a crisis. The third relates to what may be required and should be in place following a crisis.

Stage 1

The aim of stage 1 is to achieve a considered and consistent approach that can be applied at home, school and any other place a child regularly attends. Generally, it requires that all adults are familiar with policies and approaches relating to challenging behaviours, particularly any individualised plans that may exist. In a school, this may mean contributing to and/or collaborating on the development of 'risk assessments'. 'Risk assessments' usually exist where there is a known possibility of a challenging behaviour/event occurring. These may include how to respond when a child hurts another child or what to do if a child runs away. Stage 1 can also require familiarisation with information gleaned from other parties and agencies.

Both policies and approaches should be underpinned by the awareness that children with autism require reduced auditory explanations/input, especially in the management of challenging behaviours. Although this has already been noted with differing focus in other chapters and sections, its importance cannot be overstressed, and for that reason it is here given further prominence.

Without doubt, a school fit to serve all would have a whole school policy in which reducing auditory explanations/inputs was recognised as a necessary part of schooling for all visual learners. Such a whole school policy would include two essential components. These are a considered and increased cross-curricular school-wide use of visual aids and kinaesthetic approaches, and clear staff directives that have been established through whole-school training on how to respond to what is considered inappropriate/challenging behaviour/s. One possible format for such school-wide directives might be:

1. The immediate response should be non-verbal, for example stop talking altogether.

2. Maintain a sense of safety for self and others, moving oneself to a prudent closeness to the child.

3. During the process take responsibility for your own displeasure – 'I don't like xxxx', and, if the behaviour manifested is familiar, show the child the appropriate visual aid/s, for example 'No shouting!'

4. In some schools/units there may be the agreed practice of showing a visual warning, such as a 'yellow card'.

5. In some schools/units, if the behaviour re-occurs or does not show signs of cessation, there may be the agreed practice of removal of either the child or others.

6. If a child has been removed or if others have had to be removed, then before the child returns to normal task/s s/he should be visually and sequentially shown the required visual aid, for example 'Sorry'/'Return to task' or 'Sorry'/'Put right'/'Return to task'. This may be followed by a brief verbal explanation in

which the inappropriate behaviour is precisely named but the child is not condemned or alienated, for example 'I like you, but I don't like hitting'.

7. After a crisis, even if only for a few minutes, the child should always return to task or some small aspect thereof.

Stage 2

The aim of stage 2 is to consistently and calmly defuse a crisis as quickly as possible. Consistency is particularly essential where the behaviour has been sharpened and hardened by reinforcement. An approach calmly and uniformly applied will introduce and eventually imprint an alternative, positive scenario over the former, negative one.

The primary guideline for working/being with a child with autism is to reduce speech, keeping it to a minimum. Abiding by this guideline is never as important as when a child is in crisis. If a child with autism is exhibiting a challenging behaviour, the child is in crisis to some degree or another, and language should be at least minimised, at best avoided. In doing so, adults must remain calm. The child needs adults to manage her/his crisis in a considered, consistent manner, and not to raise the ante with confusing verbalisations, such as demands and instructions. If these are felt to be necessary, they should be made as much as possible through visual aids. Failing this, keep all language-based inputs as simple as possible. This approach also enables adults to focus upon being observant and reflective, gathering information for future proactive intervention plans.

Attending adults should also make space between themselves and the child, assuming as they do a non-aggressive, open stance avoiding direct eye contact: step back to a safe distance, assume an open position that is slightly turned away from the child, have arms and hands free, and lower eyes without losing focus. In doing so they need to be mindful of where they and others are, looking out for any environmental hazards to the child that could also endanger others. As the child needs space, the adult needs freedom of movement to step back and/or away. Also, both in the classroom and at home, the attending adult/s has/have responsibility towards the safety of other children/siblings. Therefore, the adult/s should be mindful of potential hazards and points of entrance/exit.

Stage 3

Stage 3 widens the scope of the event. In many ways both the preceding stages have focused on the child. In stage 1, awareness focused upon an individual child's known triggers and responses to establish a considered and consistent approach that can be applied at home, school and at any other place the child regularly attends. In stage 2, the individual child was again the centre of adult attention as his/her behaviour was calmly and consistently defused. Stage 3 now broadens out to consider the needs of all persons present at the time of the crisis before reflection and further proactive intervention can take place.

After a crisis it is common for those managing it to experience exhaustion and negative emotions. Some carers may feel the need for a break. When working as part of a team this is more likely to be possible than in the home situation or a short-staffed classroom. However, a break for those managing a crisis should be construed an imperative rather than a personnel-bound possibility. Exhaustion and negative emotions are stressors that can ultimately damage health and relationships. Therefore, in a short-staffed classroom the responsible person should have a plan for providing rest and recuperation to staff following a crisis. For example, showing the class their favourite film or having an extra free play session allows the adult witnesses to take stock, while any children who witnessed the crisis can release their own tensions in relaxing pursuits.

In the home situation it is equally important to acknowledge the effects of a crisis upon those present. Therefore, carers should consider how they will provide themselves and the other children/people possibly present with a period of rest and recuperation following a crisis. Again, this may well be putting on a well-loved film/cartoon or even an outdoor play session in a child-friendly space for the children involved, making space and time for the carer/s to reflect and de-stress. In an ideal situation the carer who was the primary manager of the crisis would have space and time away to recollect her/himself, especially if s/he felt this necessary. Particularly for family members, there can be emotional repercussions that go beyond what can be known or at the time perceived.

Nevertheless, the danger is that the aftermath is perceived as reinforcing the preceding behaviour by the child him/herself. Therefore, to avoid this, there needs to be an interlude between the crisis and the rest and recuperation period. This interlude can be seen to be part of the defusing period. It can be a period of quiet and reflection when other children/siblings return briefly to tasks they were doing. It can be a period of 'making good' in which the child assists in putting away, tidying or mending toys/objects/items disarrayed or damaged. It can be a period of recovery in which the child completes an unfinished task or just sits quietly for a given time marked by a visual countdown.

However, beyond the interlude, and the rest and recuperation periods, there is the business of reflection and reassessment for all the concerned and involved adults.

Autism, Challenging Behaviours, Transition and Change

Children with autism who often struggle with transition and change can be overwhelmed by strong emotions at these times and succumb to meltdown. However, the child with autism can be helped to understand and prepare for transitions and changes through visual, written formats, such as Gray's (1994a) Social Stories™ described above.

One such change for which all children with autism should have gentle preparation and rehearsal for is the transition from home to nursery or nursery to school. This can easily and readily be accomplished with a personalised booklet (Figure 6.6).

Now that you are a big boy it is time to go to school.

Photograph of
student.

All big boys and girls go to school.

School is different to crèche but it is okay.

It can be fun.

You will like school.

Page 1

Photograph of
school.

This is a photograph of your school.

Page 2

These are photographs of your classroom.

Outside.   Inside.

Page 3

Photograph of
desk and chair.

This is your desk and chair. This is where you will do
your work.

Page 4

Photograph of
lunch place.

This is where you will sit to eat your lunch.

Page 5

Photograph of
the Break Area.

This is where you will rest when you need a break.

Page 6

Photograph of
shared work
space

This is where you will play turn-taking games/work
with others/share toys, etc., as appropriate to
the teacher's plan.

Page 7

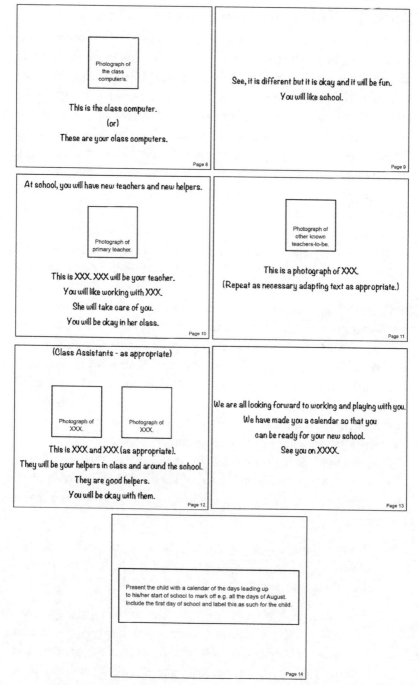

Figure 6.6 A personalised booklet for a young child with autism about to transition from home to nursery or nursery to school.

Autism, Challenging Behaviours and School Trips

There is no reason why children with autism who present with challenging behaviours cannot enjoy school trips as much as other students. Personally, although I found school trips exacting in terms of preparation and planning, they were always enjoyable occasions for students and staff. Invariably the child with autism and challenging behaviours had a calm, fun, stress-free day. This was due to thorough forethought, tight organisation and prescriptive management; ingredients that are these days essential to the success of any school trip.

To achieve these ingredients, all school trips require a responsible adult who is willing not only to research the venue but, in most instances, to visit it and familiarise him/herself with the facilities on offer and any possible risks and hazards. This reconnaisance will enable the responsible adult to thoroughly and tightly organise a day free of stress and distress for all. This organisation should include timings, such as departures and arrivals and carefully estimated toilet, rest and eating breaks that maintain as closely as possible routines the students are familiar with, regardless of the trip. It also should include positioning, such as where and how toilets can be accessed, and staff positioned to enable optimum enjoyment and a sense of freedom balanced by maximum care and supervision. Furthermore, both positioning and time planning should carefully consider where and when the students will take refreshment breaks.

There is another important task for the designated trip organiser/manager and that is the dissemination of advice to accompanying staff. For example, the following staff guidelines formed part of a booklet I prepared:

- Ensure your hands are free: only take a back pack or across-the-shoulder bag, and ensure that students carry and remember their own possessions.

- Even though you may be assigned to one, perhaps two, individual students or even a class, remember to work as part of a wider, whole team: go where the need is the greatest and do not assume that anyone will take care of a need you have identified.

- Carry an easily accessible and appropriate pack of visual aid cards, for example stop, wait, turn-taking, bus, school, walk, toilet and lunch cards.

- Older students who need to be guided should be done so as much as possible with a hand on the shoulder and/or one on the lower back rather than by holding their hand, which is socially inappropriate to their physical age, but older students may hold hands with younger ones where appropriate and helpful.

- Make the responsible adult and other adults aware of any indication of mounting stress/distress in students, because the earlier the indication the more chance there is of preventing escalation.

However, in case of escalation to a crisis, also in the same booklet was advice on crisis management, such as:

- If a student goes into crisis/meltdown, quickly assess where you are most needed. It may be one of the following:

  - Protecting others, ensuring their safety and well-being from onset to conclusion of crisis.

  - Providing a temporary shield from public glare and/or curiosity for those attempting to manage and calm the situation/student.

  However, the responsible adult may feel that the appropriate response is to ignore the behaviour/s, walking away while keeping the student in sight. If so, follow the lead.

Classroom Essentials: Layout and Practices

Given the many possible variables, such as the personality and values of the teacher, the physical dimensions of the room and the age, needs and strengths of students, classroom layouts and practices inevitably vary. However, generally, teachers who wish to provide a classroom fit for all should adhere to the common practices already outlined in previous chapters, and as much as possible provide the following areas.

An Independent Work Area

An independent work area should be equipped with a workstation or workstations depending upon the nature of the classroom, that is, a mainstream or a special education classroom. In this area the desk/s should be placed to minimise distraction and enable good, independent work practices. At these desks, students should be encouraged to work in the directionality used in their culture's reading/writing system, for example left to right in a Western reading/writing system. The individual schedules of the student/s using the area may be displayed at workstations or at a central desk. Again, it is usual for schedules to go left to right, but older and abler students may work with list-like schedules. The composition of schedules should vary depending on the developmental level and/or abilities of the individual student. However, they should have one of the following compositions:

- objects of reference, for example a crayon to represent colouring in

- photographs

- symbolic pictures or icons

- words only.

Also, starting from the youngest class, it should be the practice to use words with scheduled activities to foster the acquisition of the written word. This is particularly important with students who do not use speech and whose ability in written language is not readily recognisable or assessable because it should always be borne in mind that non-verbalisation does not necessarily equate with either a lack of ability or potential. For example, Jasmine Lee O'Neill, author of *Through the Eyes of Aliens* (2000), whom I have cited several times, despite being diagnosed as severely autistic and never having used spoken language, has in my opinion a moving, insightful and poetic mastery of written language. Moreover, in my own practice, I experienced the joy of watching young, non-verbal students using the written word to communicate their needs and wants. Therefore non-verbalisation does not necessarily equate with non-literacy.

All activities in the independent work area should have an academic or work bias, such as workbooks, alphabetical filing, matching activities or sorting activities. Also, they should have all been taught previously in, if possible, one-to-one situations in which the class teacher has observed and recorded the required degree of independence. Unfortunately, in my experience and professional opinion, this is not a task for delegation to another adult, such as a support worker. The class teacher him/herself needs to know beyond question that all independent work activities require no or little adult input/ assistance, or the very goal of these activities can be compromised. In other words, frustration and dependency can be promoted rather than reinforcing achievement and independence. Therefore, in my opinion, the responsible adult/teacher should never delegate this task.

Furthermore, all independent work activities should be designed to have a clear start and finish. This enables the student/s to know when to stop and put the activity in the finished work tray/area, and move onto the next task.

As the aim of this area is the development of sound, independent working skills, adults should never sit with or try to engage the students, other than to offer the facilitation or prompting seen necessary to keep or bring a student back on task. This may include:

- pointing to the next part of the work

- physical facilitation that reduces and then extinguishes as soon as possible

- verbally saying 'Next'

- pointing and/or verbally reminding a student what they are working for, for example 'break area' next on schedule

- applying deep pressure on shoulders to settle student/s.

A Structured Play/Hobbies Area

The purpose of a structured play/hobbies area is to extend or develop the interests of the student/s with autism. As outlined in Chapter 3, this is a very necessary part of the holistic education of these students because of the rigidity and repetitiveness of interest that they are prone to. As play and interests can become increasingly rigid and repetitive, it is important to promote developments and alterations in familiar pastime occupations and to introduce new ones. Also, as students with autism can be challenged by having to leave a favourite occupation, it is essential to teach them from an early age to start and stop play and hobbies on request or within set times and/or visual boundaries.

The structured play/hobbies area should be equipped with shelving that enables activities to be displayed and visually labelled for students to independently access and tidy away.[2] All activities are leisure or play focused, for example puzzles, sand play, matching games and sorting games. Also, as with the independent work activities, they should all have been taught and assessed previously in one-to-one situations in which the class teacher has observed the required degree of independence, and they should all have a clear start and finish, enabling the student to know where to begin and when to replace them on the shelf.

Again the structured play area, as with the independent work area, is designed to foster independence, and so adults should try not to sit with or engage the student/s other than to offer the facilitation or prompting seen necessary to keep or bring a student back on task. Again this may include:

- pointing to the next part of the work

- physical facilitation that reduces and then extinguishes as soon as possible

- verbally saying 'Next'

- pointing and/or verbally reminding a student what they are working for, for example 'break area' next on schedule

- applying deep pressure on shoulders to settle student/s.

A Break Area

This is an area essential to any classroom fit for children with autism. Therefore, the need for a break area should not be overlooked on any grounds, such as age, ability or maturity. Our students/children with autism have different stresses and stressors than our neurotypical students/children. Whereas the latter can find the playground restorative, co-operatively working with peers in class stimulating and simply chatting with others informative and sustaining, children with autism can perceive all these activities as stressful and anxiety ridden. These children more frequently need quiet, solitary times in which they can relax and unwind undisturbed by others while pursuing their own favourite occupations and interests. While neurotypical adults may perceive these activities as repetitive and banal, children/students with autism need a place and time to enjoy them free from opinion and judgement as much as neurotypical children/students need the freedom and camaraderie of the playground.

A break area must be equipped with the toys and resources students independently choose to occupy their free time with. These may include photograph albums, Disney characters, catalogues, paper, bubble wrap, toys with flashing lights and so forth.[3] Information regarding preferred toys and activities is best ascertained by a class teacher during her/his initial observations/assessment of a student, and from information gleaned from parents/carers and professionals who have recently been involved in daily hands-on care/work with the student.

Also, it is a good idea to require students to remove their shoes before entering the structured play area as this demarcates this area's time and space purpose. It also enhances the health and safety of the area, especially for times of transition from the area and times when more than one student is occupying it.

One of the most important tenets of this area is that students are not required to engage in any interaction when in it. Thus, the rule is that attending adults do not usually engage students unless addressed by the student first. It is the students' place for de-stressing. They may be counted down verbally and/or visually out of the area when their free time is up, and then handed the object or card that indicates return to schedule. Alternatively they may simply be given the schedule object or card. However, apart from these 'ending' and 'transitioning' communications, time in this area is given to students to relax and de-stress in a place where autism is respected, not ignored or chipped away at.

Also, for students with autism, a break area is a useful place during wet playtimes, provided the rules and guidelines that govern this area are consistently abided to.

However, despite its many advantages and enormous importance, a break area adds to a class teacher's duties. First, as already noted, it requires input to establish appropriately. This includes discovering through observation and play the preferred interests and hobbies of individual children. Second, it requires careful maintenance. This can be more onerous than in other classroom areas because, aiming to give zero stress to students with autism, they are not usually required to tidy up after themselves. The one exception to this is that a child may wish to keep a favourite toy in a special place. Therefore, when there are no students in the break area, class teachers, and assistants if available, need to carry out duties such as the following:

- general tidy

- mend/fix any damaged activities, such as books and catalogues

- wash, and if necessary disinfect or sterilise, toys

- replace broken toys or severely damaged activities

- straighten/fix wall displays if any.

A Practice Area

Additionally, there was another area that I found necessary in my teaching of children with autism. This was one in which skills/concepts not readily grasped, and therefore requiring more long-term input, a very gradual reduction in facilitation and/or ongoing monitoring, could be regularly revisited and practised with an adult, that is, a place where the child could achieve with support what s/he could not yet independently achieve. I built these into daily activities that I labelled 'table-top activities' and, having seen these activities modelled, support assistants were able to work on them with students in another distraction-free area of the classroom that had been set up for this work. Usually I observed the assistant sitting opposite the student modelling the task, but on occasion s/he sat behind the student providing physical facilitation, for example hand-on-hand, hand-on-wrist or hand-on-elbow.

Other Areas and Considerations

Furthermore, while I strongly recommend that these four areas be considered essential, the purposes/functions of other parts of a classroom need to be clear, visible and considered for students with autism. For example, the place where one-to-one work with the teacher occurs, usually the 'teacher's desk', can be labelled 'Work with Teacher'. However, this is not the traditional 'teacher's desk'. This is not the teacher's place laden with the teacher's belongings. It is a place equipped with the essential requirements for a teacher to work with his/her students, primarily on a one-to-one basis. So, while teachers' desks normally command all-round classroom views, for students who are distracted by sights and/or sounds it may be necessary to position them facing the teacher or a wall that is free from distracting/stimulating displays. In my own teaching practice, I found it easier to work with students sitting beside me, directly facing a wall. While from my position I could turn and observe the other students and attending staff, the student working with me faced the wall while being screened by my body from classroom activities. Thus, I could teach the cognitive/academic teaching targets identified in individualised education plans with minimal distraction while maintaining an overall classroom perspective.

Another area that requires clarity, visibility and consideration of the needs of students with autism is the group area or space. Given the spatial limitations of the average classroom, this is usually a multi-purpose area where the following activities may all take place:

- morning greeting, news, weather and so on

- whole class instruction and inputs

- lunch

- board games

- art and craft activities.

Regardless of the breadth of activities, this area can be labelled 'Group Work' to enable students with autism to understand its general purpose/function.

Notes

1. This behavioural rule/code uses a metaphor that a young person must first understand and make sense of.
2. Younger students or students with emotional needs may have independent work and structured play areas integrated to reduce movement and/or stress.
3. Break areas for older students are equally essential and should be appropriately equipped to meet their needs and interests with the likes of large cushions, comfortable chairs, comic books and individualised audio files to be used with headphones on an available device.

Chapter 7

SENSORY AND PHYSICAL NEEDS

Introduction

Since the 1990s many people with autism, workers and researchers in the field have argued that sensory needs should be recognised as a significant feature of autism. Finally, in 2013 the *Diagnostic and Statistical Manual of Mental Disorders, Fifth Edition* included hyper and hypo-sensitivity and reaction to sensory input, and extraordinary interest in the sensory features of the environment, as part of the diagnosis of autism.

Working in this field, I fully welcomed and endorsed this long-awaited recognition of sensory needs, and the inclusion of self-harm behaviours and physical characteristics as recognisable features of autism. The latter, as I had often observed, includes odd gait, clumsiness and other idiosyncratic motor behaviours. Self-harm includes head banging and self-biting.

Thus, in this chapter I will discuss these, along with a separate section concerning the visual sensory orientation and needs of children with autism.

Sensory Needs

Frequently within my teaching practice I met children with autism who also had sensory needs. These included:

- the need for deep pressure especially at times of stress and/or anxiety

- the need for movement even when working

- the need to reduce external auditory input by covering the ears in some way

- the need to touch, stroke and smell substances, textures, colours and so forth

- the experience of discomfort and/or distress with touch, including certain fabrics, textures and pressures.

In my work with children with autism it was also evident that some children were primarily hyper-sensitive while others were largely hypo-sensitive. This is a very important distinction that describes two very different poles of what for some, especially occupational therapists, consider to be a large part of autism. Hyper-sensitivity and hypo-sensitivity are terms associated with what some term a sensory integration disorder (SID) and others a sensory processing disorder (SPD). These terms are commonly interchanged and confused, but the first is principally used to describe the theory and intervention treatment advocated by Dr (Anna) Jean Ayres (1920–1988) and the latter to define and describe what is considered a sensory processing disorder.

Ayres was an occupational therapist and a developmental psycho-logist who coined the term 'sensory integration dysfunction' in the 1960s. She went on to write several books on the subject, including one she co-authored with Jeff Robbins, and is perhaps most well known for *Sensory Integration and the Child* (Ayres and Robbins 1979). Ayres also went on to develop assessment tests to be used in the identification of a sensory integration disorder. However, her theory and conclusions remain controversial today.

Furthermore, whilst the distinction between sensory integration and processing is important to some within the field, the controversy over the theories and conclusions of sensory integration/processing are not restricted to Ayres's work alone. For example, many expected sensory integration/processing to be included in the DSM-5 as a separate disorder but were disappointed.

Nevertheless, despite this controversy, within my own practice I frequently met children with autism who had sensory needs. In doing so I came to agree with many occupational therapists and other professionals that these needs could be broadly divided into hyper- and hypo-sensitivity. In brief, children who are hyper-sensitive can be over-sensitive to sights, sounds, textures, tastes, smells and other sensory inputs that are experienced as overloads. Meanwhile, children who are hypo-sensitive are under-sensitive to environmental sensory inputs. These polar conditions manifest in different ways.

Children who are hyper-sensitive may react strongly and/or negatively to loud noises. Additionally, they may be distracted by sounds that for others are ignorable background noises. In this way it was my experience that children who are hyper-sensitive can give priority to preferred background sounds over an adult voice that they are expected to tune into. For example, I observed children focusing in on external noises, such as those made by lawnmowers, dogs and motorbikes, at the expense of classroom dialogues/discussions.

Moreover, they may attune to smells that others overlook. For example, one child I worked with seemed to be experiencing a fear of dentists. This may be considered a common enough fear, but as it turned out it was the smell of the examination room, not the situation itself, that was causing his stress and distress. Once his strong reaction to the smells of the examination room had been observed and noted, actions to counteract them were taken and resolutions were found. At the same time, I have used hyper-sensitivity to smell to relax or calm children with autism. For example, another child I worked with had a passion for the smell of toast. Many new places were happily accessed because he was greeted by wafts of toasting bread!

Nevertheless, hyper-sensitivity generally brings with it distress for the child and stress for his/her carers. For example, children who are hyper-sensitive may have an aversion to touch, including the touch of familiar adults. Clearly such a hyper-sensitivity can create barriers to intimacy for children with autism while distressing those who love them. Also, in an acute form, fear of touch can become fear of the closeness of others. Children with this fear struggle in crowds, playgrounds and a host of other environments in which proximity to others is the norm. For them, exacerbated anxiety about their own safety can become paramount, and the simple threat of being bumped into can become the trigger to panic attacks.

Furthermore, their over-sensitivity to sights, sounds, textures, tastes, smells and other sensory inputs can make outings to places other children enjoy an overwhelming, nightmarish experience. Even school and other familiar places may not always prove safe havens to these children who can react with 'meltdowns'.

Ryan (2010, paragraph 6:1) describes a 'meltdown' as 'an intense response to overwhelming situations'. From this description, it is clearly important to recognise that autism meltdowns are not the same as temper tantrums, although those witnessing them may assume that they are. Temper tantrums usually occur when the wishes and/or wants of a child are thwarted. Also, they can be reinforced and become learned behaviours by which children demand and achieve their own way. However, meltdowns have three distinctive features. First, they occur when a person with autism is completely and utterly overwhelmed by a situation. Second, the person with autism must be finding it difficult and/or impossible to communicate her/his stress and distress. Third, because of the two preceding features, the person with autism loses control of their own behaviour. This loss of control, like a temper tantrum, can be expressed verbally or physically, or both. Loss of verbal control can take the form of shouting, screaming or crying. Loss of physical control has many forms, such as hitting, kicking or biting. Undeniably, none of this differentiation between an autism meltdown and a temper tantrum excludes the reality that a child with autism may also be prone to temper tantrums. Therefore, the onus clearly rests with the attending adult/s to recognise the cause/s and the difference/s.

Fortunately, however, the management of both temper tantrums and meltdowns share some basic, similar strategies. These are predominantly:

- With a meltdown it is important not to judge the child as those witnessing it may be doing, unaware that the child has autism. With a temper tantrum it is important not to react emotionally, although that is exactly what the tantrum is designed to make the parent/carer do! Clearly these similar strategies are concerned with retaining a level of objective detachment so that considered responses are possible.

- Children with autism presenting with a meltdown and those exhibiting a temper tantrum require patience, reduced auditory input and time. In neither scenario is the child capable of inputting any more information. In other words, in both cases the child needs a recovery time, the length of which is individual to the child and situation. It cannot and should not be rushed by adults watching clocks for the next scheduled lesson or action they have planned.

- In both scenarios the child and witnesses need space. The child needs a space to be safe and calmed in, while those witnessing either a meltdown or a temper tantrum may need a space in which they can be safe from verbal and/or physical behaviours. In a public place this may require asking people to move on, not to intervene or even not to stand and stare. On initial occasions, taking the control of the situation in this way may be personally challenging for an adult, and clearly it is only possible if the adult/s has/have retained the detached distance recommended in strategy one. However, all these strategies become easier and more spontaneous with practice as carers develop their individual resources and their own personal means of delivery. For example, Rachel Pinney, the creator of 'Children's Hours/Special Times', in her book *Bobby: Breakthrough of an Autistic Child* (1983), printed off small, postcard-size explanations stating that the child in her care had autism and asking bystanders to simply move on without intervening or staring. So, as well as not judging the child, do not judge yourself and, as well as giving the child time, allow yourself time to learn and master strategies.

- While both situations require the attending adult/s to make a safe space between the child and others, the space created should be quiet and subdued to reduce sensory input/overload. For example, turn off any music, lights, computers and televisions, move along any superfluous bystanders and stop talking or limit your own speech to simple, repetitious phrases that you know soothe the child.

Fortunately, in a manner of speaking, meltdowns are usually preceded by determinable signs that are sometimes described as the 'rumble stage'. These are individual to the child and cover a vast array of visible signs that include both decreasing movement until extreme stillness is accomplished and increasing aggravated rocking and/or pacing. Some more vocal children may resort to seeking calming reassurance through repetitive questioning. However, if left unrecognised as a pre-meltdown strategy, 'rumble' behaviours often prove counteractive as they can aggravate already inflamed situations. All the same, at the 'rumble stage' there is still the opportunity to avert a meltdown. Therefore, it is very important for attending adult/s to know and monitor the individualistic pre-meltdown behaviours/strategies of any child in their care, and respond to these timely and appropriately.

The method commonly recommended to identify and thereby eradicate or minimise the causes/triggers of meltdowns is record taking, such as the keeping of a diary. One record-keeping method that I found effectively identified pre-meltdown behaviours and meltdown triggers is the 'Antecedents Behaviour Consequence Chart' (the 'ABC of Behaviour'), also known as the 'Antecedents Chart'. ABC stands for antecedent–behaviour–consequence and refers to an observational chart used to collect and correlate data regarding challenging behaviours and their triggers and consequences. Over my many years of working in the field of special/additional needs I have seen and used many versions of the 'ABC of Behaviour'. Tables 7.1 and 7.2 show but two examples.

Table 7.1 Example 1 of an Antecedent Behaviour Consequence (ABC of Behaviour) Chart, also commonly known as an 'Antecedents Chart'.

Date	Time	Anticedent	Behaviour	Consequence	Function

Table 7.2 Example 2 of an 'Antecedents Chart'.

Day and time	What did ____ do?	What do you think provoked it?	Where did it happen?	What did you do?	What happened because of your efforts?

In the management of challenging behaviours, these charts are particularly useful in the recognition of the behavioural signs that precede meltdowns and the triggers that cause them. For example, the child with hyper-sensitivity may start to rock with increasing rapidity when in a music lesson in which someone is making a screechy noise with an instrument. If no intervention occurs, this may eventually lead to a meltdown in which s/he screams, lashes out at others and/or runs out of the room. Clearly the trigger here was the aggravating sound, while the 'rumble stage' was characterised by the rocking that rapidly grew in intensity.

Additionally, it is important to note that not all meltdowns are caused by sensory overloads. There are other causes all occasioned by anxiety and distress. Amongst these, disturbances to routines and familiar structures figure strongly. As discussed in previous chapters, predictable routines and regular structures are very important to children with autism. Deviating or altering them can cause extreme distress that may culminate in a meltdown. For example, simply taking a class out on a spontaneous nature walk may be an exciting, fun event for the neurotypical students in a class, but for a student with autism it can be a nightmare. Even at the expense of missing the perfect day for such an event, I strongly argue such ventures should be delayed until the child and support staff are suitably prepared with the necessary visual aids, Social Story™ and so forth. If not, in frightening distress, unable to communicate and with intensifying fear, a child with autism may be overwhelmed and ultimately lose control to some primal struggle to return the world to normality.

Moreover, as an 'ABC Chart' is used to observe and interpret information over several sessions by noting behaviours and the events that precede and follow them, it can also be useful in differentiating between temper tantrums and overwhelming sensory inputs. Consider the previous example of the child with hyper-sensitivity in a music lesson who reacted with rocking that built up to screaming, lashing out and/or running away: the perceived trigger was the screechy noise being made by the musical instrument. However, a child having a temper tantrum because s/he wanted the instrument another child was playing may have reacted with the same challenging behaviours. Therefore, it is in the observations of the preceding events that the differentiation is possible, for example was the rocking simply preceded by the onset of the noise or by something else, such as the instrument being given to another child?

Fortunately, having observed and noted the behaviours exhibited at the 'rumble stage', there are strategies that can be used to prevent the acceleration into meltdown. Again, these strategies are individual to a child. For example, some children may respond well to distraction/ diversion, others to time out or even music, while others relax by accessing favourite items, such as toys. However, the most important strategy of all is for attending adult/s to remain calm while reacting quickly, and reacting quickly includes noting and eradicating any potential triggers.

Meanwhile, children who are hypo-sensitive may take undue risks, lacking sensitivity and awareness of environmental dangers and hazards. This may be exacerbated by a high tolerance or even an indifference to pain. Also, needing more stimulation to satiate their sensory needs, they may be sensation-seekers, that is, 'sensory-seekers'. This may manifest in ignoring personal boundaries and standing too close to others or even in a constant touching and/or stroking of people and inanimate objects. Both such behaviours may culminate in more severe inappropriate behaviours. However, generally, these children can appear the clumsy and unco-ordinated invaders of the personal space of others. They can be perpetual movers, accidentally hurting other children as they hurtle around in both indoor and outdoor environments. Also, they may constantly take foolhardy risks, oblivious to dangers that others clearly see.

Therefore, it is evident that it is in the best interest of every child with autism who is displaying sensory sensitivity that consideration of which pole they 'predominantly inhabit' should be given as part of their educational assessment.

I have written 'predominantly inhabit' because there are clearly children with autism who have 'feet in both camps'. In other words, they may have some senses that are hyper-sensitive and others that are hypo-sensitive. Some children may even seem to present with one sense fluctuating between hyper-sensitivity and hypo-sensitivity. This latter phenomenon has been particularly observed in children with Asperger's syndrome (AS), now called mild autism. Therefore, each child and each sense needs to be individually considered.

Furthermore, when dealing with sensory needs and resulting behaviours, it should be appreciated that these arise from deep-seated impulses and needs. Like infants born with addictions to drugs or adult cravings for nicotine, children presenting with sensory needs require understanding, respect and compassion. Requiring that they disappear immediately or removing total access to expression is tantamount to 'cold turkey' treatments. Equally, scolding and punishing children with sensory needs may simply frustrate them and lead some into subterfuge. These methods can only put children and/or adults in corners of frustration, distress and/or failure. In other words, it is essential that these needs are seen to control the child rather than to see the child as in control of the needs.

So, how best to deal with these needs?

Managing Sensory Needs

People/children with autism have themselves given us the key insight into how we should manage sensory needs. Frequently the expression of need changes with time and development. In other words, the same need may be present but its expression is different. Ultimately, we have two ways of managing sensory needs. We can either saturate the need or seek to redirect it into a more appropriate expression. The choice of approach is dependent on the individuality of the expressed need and the child. For example, a child needing deep pressure may present with behaviours such as:

- pressing forehead

- squeezing others tightly

- rocking/fidgeting in seat

- leaning heavily on supporting structures or other people

- some forms of self-harm, such as biting or head banging.

In these instances, providing deep pressure and thereby saturating the need can reduce movement, anxiety and challenging behaviour. This can be done by simply applying pressure to the shoulders or the back area; wrapping up tightly as with newborn infants in weighted blankets or other available, heavy material, such as a rug; or giving deep-pressure massage strokes.

Perhaps the most well-known story about a person needing 'deep pressure' is the story of Temple Grandin and her 'hug box' also known as the 'hug machine', the 'squeeze box' or even the 'squeeze machine'. Despite craving the stimulation of deep pressure, as a young child Grandin felt overwhelmed when hugged. Then, on a visit to the ranch of an aunt, Grandin observed the way cattle were confined in a 'squeeze chute' for their inoculations. She also noted the calming effect this had on some cattle and decided that something similar might help her own hyper-sensitivity. So she designed a prototype 'squeeze box' for her own personal use from which an industry of 'hug boxes' emerged. Despite initial controversy, the 'hug box' has become an established therapy for some children/persons with autism. It works by having two side-boards with thick, soft padding between which the user lies or squats while controlling an air compressor that applies an even, deep pressure to his/her body.

Meanwhile, other children with autism may appear hyper-active. They may fidget or not sit for required periods of time. In these instances, when independently working or playing it may be possible to let children assume whatever stance they need to complete tasks successfully. However, it may not be classroom-appropriate to allow them to pace or move about excessively. Therefore, sandwiching stationary activities such as group times and work tasks between brief periods of physical activity can enable greater concentration at necessary sessions. For example, whole body activities such as bouncing on trampolines, peanut/gym balls, running, skipping, swinging and jumping can reduce hyper-activity for small, required periods of sandwiched time.

Over the years, I also met students with a variety of other sensory needs. Sometimes these were dependent on the individual child's stage of cognitive development. For example, a child diagnosed with autism and moderate general learning disabilities may have smell as the predominant sense. However, to assume that sensory need correlates with cognitive ability can be a mistake because I worked with students with all levels of ability who had oral/mouthing needs/compulsions. These needs are deep seated, may have stress triggers and are hard to eradicate because, like water, they will adapt to their environment and somehow find expression.

Also, if the underlying trigger cannot be identified and managed, then redirecting the need towards a more appropriate, acceptable expression is the only viable, stress-free, long-term action for families and professionals. For example, in the case of a child whose dominant sense is smell, one strategy may be to encourage him to use tissues infused with different smells. At first redirection can take high levels of adult monitoring and intervention, but these can be gradually reduced as the child adapts the behaviour.

Physical Needs

In my teaching practice every child I worked with had some observable level of need relating to balance and co-ordination. As many adults noted, this may well have been simply because I have yet to meet a child with or without autism in whom I could not identify some level of need in this area! Whilst agreeing, I would argue that, in my experience, balance and co-ordination needs are more visible in children with autism. More specifically, I often observed these needs in the gait of children with autism. They frequently walked with straight, unbending leg movements and experienced difficulties synchronising whole-body movements. Therefore, I strongly argue that physical exercises aimed at improving co-ordination and balance should be included in the daily timetable of all children with autism.

My awareness of a relationship between physical movement and the learning needs and potential of children first began in the 1970s when I learnt of the hypothesis that early movement and learning are correlated. Initially this hypothesis was based on a claim that crawling on all fours had an impact upon cognitive development, particularly relating to reading and spelling. This argument continues to be debated despite many cultural studies. These studies seem to raise the question of nature versus nurture in their evidence of cultural practices either encouraging or bypassing crawling as a significant developmental stage. However, contrasting research, usually undertaken by advocates of this theory, does support the view that crawling plays a role in the development of strength, balance, spinal alignment, visual-spatial skills and even socio-emotional development; and this has led some Western professionals to advocate the importance of crawling, recommending that parents encourage their children to crawl on all fours for brief periods of time every day.

The theory is based on crawling being a 'whole-body' movement. This simply means that when infants crawl they use their arms and legs to lift and transport their torsos off and across the floor. Also, in this way an infant is working against gravity while developing the strength and dexterity of muscles throughout the body. Moreover, whilst this whole-body movement is clearly having an impact on gross motor skills, it is also argued that there are subtler influences taking place because the required extension and weight bearing of the wrists develops the arching that is crucial to the fine motor skill development of the hands. Then, beyond the impact upon the gross and fine motor skills, it is further contended that crawling is significant in the developmental process of visual skills. This argument is based upon the fact that as infants crawl they are required to alternate between distant and near vision, repeatedly adjusting the focus of the eyes. This repeated adjustment of focus trains eye muscles and develops what is known as 'binocular vision'. Binocular vision is the ability to synchronise the eyes. It is an essential prerequisite for future reading and writing. Additionally, as crawling is a whole-body movement, not only must the eyes work together but also both hemispheres of the brain and the body, that is, the right brain/body with the left brain/body. This cross-lateral integration is the basis of motor co-ordination. Finally, there are even those who also argue that crawling has a part to play in socio-emotional development. They base this predominantly on the premise that infants supposedly only develop a fear of heights after they begin to crawl, that is, after they have begun to move about independently of others with a developing sense of their own determination, autonomy and freedom underpinned by goals they have set.

From such initial theories and studies emerged a range of interventions that offer different approaches to improving co-ordination and balance. Although each school may argue for its 'uniqueness', for me they are branches of one tree that shares common historical roots. These roots are in the ancient Eastern tradition of yoga and its connection with the much more recent field of kinesiology. Yoga combines physical movements and poses with meditation and controlled breathing, while kinesiology is the study of muscles and the movement of the body. We owe the initial development from one to the other to Dr George Goodheart, who founded applied kinesiology in 1964 based on a model of muscle testing developed in the 1930s by a husband and wife team called Kendal and Kendal. Muscle testing is now used in orthopaedic medicine.

At the next step in the process, developments were not simply linear but amplified. Also, while the amplification claims of 'uniqueness' are questionable, the claims of some for validity have been plagued by more controversy than others. Nevertheless, given the persistent shelf-life of some of these developments and approaches, it is important to examine them in some detail.

Psychomotor Patterning

My starting point is with the intervention most plagued by controversy: psychomotor patterning. In 1955 Doman and Delacato founded the Institutes for the Achievement of Human Potential (IAHP), offering a new treatment for people with learning disabilities, brain injuries and other cognitive difficulties. This treatment was psychomotor patterning, sometimes referred to as the Doman–Delacato technique. It has several different forms that include the Delacato method, the Doman method and developmental reflexive rehabilitation. It is primarily based on the theory that ontogeny (the stages through which organisms develop from single cell to maturity) recapitulates phylogeny (the evolutionary history of the species). In the case of psychomotor patterning, the early neurodevelopmental stages that take a child from crawling, to creeping, through crude walking to the final mature walking of a human being are believed to mirror the evolution of our ancestors from amphibians to reptiles and finally mammals. The theory holds that 'developmental disabilities', of which autism is seen to be one, ranging from mild to severely profound, are caused by an individual's failure to develop through the proper phylogenetic stages. From this premise it is argued that the brain injury can be resolved by moving the body in specific patterns, which provides feedback to the damaged brain, helping it to heal itself through a process of 'rewiring'. In other words, when one moves repeatedly in the manner of the current stage, proper development through that phylogenetic stage is stimulated, and only when a stage is mastered can one move on to the next. For example, at the stage called 'homolateral crawling', an individual is required to crawl by turning their head to one side while flexing the arm and leg of that side, and extending the arm and leg of the opposite side. Those unable to do this independently are repeatedly moved by several adults for approximately 5 minutes, four times per day. Also, in the full treatment programme advocated, this exercise regime was combined with sensory stimulation, breathing exercises aimed at increasing the flow of oxygen to the brain, and physical restrictions and facilitation designed to promote hemispheric dominance, that is, left- or right-brain dominance.

Psychomotor patterning has been rigorously subjected to many controlled trials and all have concluded that it serves no therapeutic role. However, it continues to be used by some advocates, and its core concept that unresolved, residual deficits in early movement or reflexes adversely affect cognitive development and learning ability has had an influence on other, more accepted therapies.

Brain Gym

In the 1970s kinesiology under the guidance of Paul Dennison and later in collaboration with Gail Hargrove, who became his wife, evolved into another therapeutic approach now commonly known as 'Brain Gym' (Dennison and Dennison 1994 [1989]). Brain Gym is also known as 'educational kinesiology'.

The core principle of Brain Gym is that moving with intention leads to optimal learning. There are 26 intentional movements that are meant to reflect the movements of the first years of life when a child is learning to co-ordinate his/her eyes, ears, hands and whole body. Advocates claim that the repetition of these 26 movements stimulates the brain, enabling repatterning through the creation of neural pathways. This then allows the brain to function at a higher level, performing tasks that were once difficult.

Although Brain Gym does not suffer from the same negative controversy as psychomotor patterning, it is not without its critics, and clearly there are conceptual similarities, such as repetition of movement leading to release, repatterning and development. Nevertheless, the actual science behind it has roots in a well-accepted and approved therapeutic treatment of stroke victims. Physiotherapists and occupational therapists commonly advocate the repeated use of limbs. They contend that moving the body in repeated patterns stimulates the healthy brain to take over the work previously done by the stroke-damaged portion of the brain, creating new neural pathways as it does so. Moreover, this theory has been scientifically supported by research findings and is highly recommended by prestigious organisations such as the National Institute of Neurological Disorders and Stroke (NINDS) in the USA:

> There is a strong consensus among rehabilitation experts that the most important element in any rehabilitation program is carefully directed, well-focused, repetitive practice – the same kind of practice used by all people when they learn a new skill, such as playing the piano or pitching a baseball. (NINDS 2014, p.2)

Neurodevelopmental Theorists

From the emerging belief that early movement impacts upon the development of the growing child came research into what are termed 'the primitive reflexes'. The primitive reflexes are a group of behavioural motor responses that can be observed in early development within the womb and in infancy, but which are subsequently inhibited as the child grows. In other words, they are part of a broad group of reflexes that are developmental, and as such they normally become redundant as the child learns and refines more sophisticated skills. Put more precisely, neonates and infants go through various stages of development that ensure both physical and cognitive growth, and during these stages they perform certain physical movements that help them to progress successfully through each stage. Moreover, these physical movements are repeatedly performed to build the muscle and create the neuron pathways to the higher thinking brain until they become integrated within broader patterns of behaviour. Once integration has occurred, they become redundant and are usually inhibited. Recognised primitive reflexes include the rooting and the Moro reflex.

The rooting reflex emerges in utero around the 24th to the 28th week to be fully present at the time of birth. Combined with the suck and swallow reflexes, the rooting reflex is clearly present to enable survival, as it ensures that the newborn turns toward the food source and opens her/his mouth wide enough to latch on to either breast or bottle. The rooting reflex is said to be at its strongest in the hours following birth and is usually inhibited around the third or fourth month of life (Goddard 1996). However, neurodevelopmental theorists contend that children in whom it does not diminish may experience:

- sensitive and immature oral responses in and around the mouth

- the tongue remaining too far forward in the mouth, interfering with swallowing and chewing when solid food is introduced

- excessive dribbling

- speech and articulation needs

- hand motor skills being adversely affected as the residual reflex continues to affect the hands.[1]

The Moro reflex was first noted by Moro in 1918. It emerges in utero around the ninth week to be fully present at the time of birth. It consists of a sudden symmetrical movement of the arms upwards, away from the body, while the hands open and freeze for a moment before gradually returning down and across the body into a clasping posture. This is accompanied by a sudden inhalation of breath. It is considered a response to a sudden, unexpected noise, movement, environmental change, pain or even rough handling. Thus it is an involuntary reaction to threat. As such it is our earliest form of the 'fight' or 'flight' response clearly present as a tool for our survival, arousing or summoning assistance. However, neurodevelopmental theorists contend that the following are some of the conditions children with an unextinguished Moro reflex may experience:

- problems with the vestibular system, such as travel sickness and poor balance and co-ordination

- oculomotor, visual-perceptual and possible auditory confusion problems due to hyper-sensitivity to bright, loud and abrasive sensory stimuli

- allergies and lowered immunity difficulties, such as asthma, eczema or frequent ear, nose and throat infections

- low stamina

- low adaptability to transition and change.

Moreover, from the theory of the primitive reflexes arose the neurodevelopmental hypothesis that learning and behaviour can be blocked by unintegrated primitive reflexes, and that integrating the appropriate reflex will open higher thinking pathways. Therefore, organisations with deviations on this common theme of integrating primitive reflexes have arisen. What they all commonly share is the conviction that (1) daily exercises performed for just a few minutes per day for (2) a specific period will result in (3) visible change at (4) any age beyond the early childhood stage. Claims of positive, visible change include balance, concentration, cognitive development and academic achievement generally.

A Classroom/Home Amalgamation of Exercises

Therefore, within the classroom and as settling exercises for homework, there was a small series of exercises that I used and recommended for children in primary schools. These were drawn from both my Brain Gym and neurodevelopmental training. Although I accept that the evidence of their appropriateness and success is still open to question and investigation, I remain convinced that they do no harm, and more significantly have a role to play in the education of all children. More specifically, I believe that in my teaching practice I observed improvements in children's balance and co-ordination, in the calming of behaviours and the settling to work. They are as follows, along with some of the simple phrases used to encourage and direct the students.

Brain Buttons

Put one hand on your tummy and the other hand at the top of your chest – and rub. Keep the hand on your tummy still. Rub with the hand on your chest. Good rubbing!

Now, change hands. Keep the hand on your tummy still and rub with the hand on your chest. Good rubbing!

Hands Out to the Side

Stretch them down and shake with the whole arm. Good shaking!

Cross-Crawling

Two hands on the tummy; one over the other. Now, up to the shoulder, down to the knee and back. (Repeat until three actions have been carried out on both sides.) Good work! Well done!

Tendon Flexing

Put one foot over the other knee. Put one hand (same side as the knee being used) on your toes and one hand on the knee (same side as the foot being used). Now push the foot forward, one, two, three; pull it back, one, two, three. (Repeat twice on both sides.) Good work! Well done!

Stand Up

Good standing!

Balancing 1

Feet flat on the floor, a little apart and straight ahead. Now up on your toes and down; up on your toes and down; last time, up on your toes and down. Good balancing!

Balancing 2

Now back on your heels and forward; back on your heels and forward; last time, back on your heels and forward. Great balancing!

Balancing 3

Feet flat on the floor, a little apart and straight ahead. Now lift one leg and hold to a count of five: one, two, three, four, five. Well done! Good balancing! (Repeat on the other leg.)

Homo-Lateral Movement

Feet flat on the floor, a little apart and straight ahead. Now leg and hand up (same side of the body, leg to right angle like leg of a table and hand like bouncing a ball) and down. Other side, leg and hand up and down. Change sides, leg and hand up and down. (Repeat three times on each side of the body.) Good exercising!

Cross-Lateral Movement

Feet flat on the floor, a little apart and straight ahead. Now leg up and hand over and back across (opposite hand tapping knee). (Repeat three times on each side as with the homo-lateral movement exercise above.) Good exercising!

Cross-Overs

Sit down; put your feet flat on the floor, a little apart and straight ahead. Now cross your ankles and cross your hands on your chest. Head up, eyes down. Relax. (This is a silent time lasting up to a couple of minutes – more if possible.)

Finish

Now, uncross your ankles. Uncross your arms and hands to the side. Now put your fingertips together in front of your tummy and slowly raise your hands up, up, slowly, up, past your mouth, past your eyes, until they are over your head. Now wait, and wait, and wait. Now slowly open your arms and bring them down out to the side. Slowly down, and down, and down, until they are stretched down at your side. Now put your two hands on your tummy, one over the other, and breathe in. Fill the tummy up with air and hold. Now breathe out and hold. Now breathe in again…etc., three times. Exercises finished! Good exercising! Well done, you did it!

Visual Orientation and Needs

No chapter regarding the sensory needs of children with autism would be complete without some discussion about visual orientation and needs. In my practice this area provoked much personal and professional interest. Visual idiosyncrasies are highly common in children with autism and as such form part of the behaviourist checklist that constitutes the current assessment process. These behaviours include absence of eye contact, staring at spinning objects or light, fleeting peripheral glances, sideways viewing and a sense of difficulty attending visually, especially to other people. Moreover, there is ongoing speculation as to whether these behaviours result from or are the cause of children with autism using visual information in what neurotypical people may consider an inefficient or erroneous manner. For example, an inability to integrate central and peripheral vision may make it difficult to follow moving objects with the eyes. This is believed to be the root cause of why many children with autism do not look directly at moving objects but instead simply scan them or look off to the side of them. Alternatively, it may also be an important factor in why some children with autism ignore peripheral vision and remain fixated on a central focal point for what the neurotypical would consider long periods of time. It may also explain the observed difficulty of not being able to maintain visual attention as the co-ordination needed may be experienced as demanding, stressful or even impossible.

Therefore, how this inability to co-ordinate central and peripheral vision impacts upon the individual child with autism should be given due regard during the undertaking of any educational assessment. For example, when undertaking assessments of students, I observed individuals who focused in on the left or right sides of pages, and others who focused in on the top or bottom. Clearly where this vision was exclusive or fixated had implications for what the student gleaned, understood and learned. In the final analysis, the primary inability to co-ordinate central and peripheral vision has an impact upon the processing of visual information, and when visual processing is disrupted, other abilities are also affected, such as cognitive and motor/physical.

Note

1. The rooting reflex is strongly connected to the palmar reflex. The palmar reflex is when a light touch on the palm of the hand of a newborn will make the fingers close. As many parents and nursery staff know, gently stroking the palms of an infant's hands will encourage the sucking reflex. This shows the powerful relationship between the palmar/hand reflex and the rooting/sucking reflex.

Chapter 8

LITERACY AND MATHEMATICAL APPROACHES

Introduction

In this chapter I discuss literacy and mathematical approaches and strategies through the lenses of left-brain theories and my teaching experiences. Although I explore the implications of being left-brain thinkers for both subjects, the literacy section focuses upon how left-brain thinking affects the child's learning, while the mathematical section focuses upon how best to impart the subject content to children with autism.

Left-Brain Thinkers

If we follow the line of enquiry that indicates neurological differences in the left-brain hemisphere of adults with autism, then we must look at the qualities of this hemisphere in the appropriate education of children with autism. The left brain is called the Logic Brain because it takes a linear and sequential approach. The following qualities are considered symptomatic of left-brain dominant people:

- processing from pieces to whole

- interest in details of sounds and pictures

- focus on the specific rather than the general

- linear, sequential thinking

- step-by-step processing, thinking and working

- logical

- planned and structured

- preference for printing rather than cursive script

- use of words/verbalisation in learning is highly functional and/or used to block out distraction rather than a tool of comprehension

- enjoyment of logical, clinical analysis and processing

- time consciousness.

Loosely combining these with our current understanding of autism, we can arrive at the following implications for teaching of literacy and mathematics for children with autism in school. These equally hold for supporting them with school work at home:

- Use predominantly visual approaches.

- As the word autism implies, the child with autism is 'self-bound'; therefore all teaching should begin with the self. For example, a first reading book should have photographs of the child and their immediate family.

- Always build from the concretely functional to the abstract. Equally, always counter-check that the knowable is rooted in the doable.

- Use simple, repetitious structures that enable the gradual introduction of abstract words or concepts. For example, 'This is xxxx' can become 'This is xxxx and xxxx.'

- Use books with simple, repetitious presentation styles.

- Use simple, repetitious story books with finger following and shared reading techniques.

Literacy

Applying these insights into the development of literacy, clear indications as to the most appropriate approaches and methods emerge.

Reading and Book Skills

- Initially the child is most likely to focus on the feature most visually interesting to him/her on a page. This is usually the picture, not the print. Then, even within the picture, the child will 'home in' on what is personally the most interesting detail/s of the picture rather than the whole picture and its meaning.

- The child is highly likely to have analysis processing needs. It is appropriate to allow this need to be satisfied before pursuing your own aims: give the child processing time.

- Visual recall rather than meaning is more likely to dominate. This means that, while the child may develop word recognition easily, the main teaching focus will most likely need to be the meaning of text.

- When understanding text, the child is likely to give a sequential recall of explicit events rather than insightful comprehension of implicit meanings.

- The child with autism needs the meaning of text to be taught from the functional to the abstract. For example, *s/he is* doing/looking/carrying/going *because xxxx. S/he will be* happy/sad *because xxxx.*

- Embrace repetition! The child with autism loves it. It is known and safe. This brings comfort. Use repetition as an aid to learning.

Writing
Handwriting

- A child with autism will focus on the details, 'homing in' on interesting features. This may lead to a 'hieroglyphic' writing style, that is, with additional curves, circles, squiggles and so forth.

- A child with autism will most likely prefer print over the cursive, whole-word style of writing.

- As a visual learner, letter shapes can be readily imprinted before the teaching of correct letter formation has begun. Visual learning is highly likely to take predominance over kinaesthetic. This may be impossible to correct with rigidity of thinking.

Creative Writing

- The child with autism is highly likely to focus on details. In this case it may be keywords with omission of the incidental small words, such as 'a' and 'the'.

- Given the tendency to sequential thought and concrete understanding, the writing of a child with autism may lack creativity. It is highly likely to have a linear, sequential composition relating actual events from the initial event to the final one.

- Written compositions are highly likely to be repetitious.

Spelling

In the teaching and learning of spelling, children with autism predominantly require a look–cover–write approach rather than a phonetic decoding one. This is because the preferred learning style of the left hemisphere is a visual one, and children with autism are renowned for being visual learners. So whilst our mainstream primary classrooms have strongly and effectively taken on the principle that the basis of good reading is phonological awareness and knowledge, children with autism require what was once called the 'look-and-say' methods. This applies across all areas of literacy:

- reading: look-and-say rather than phonetic or contextual approaches to learning

- writing: look-and-write rather than kinaesthetic/motor or auditory approaches to learning

- spelling: look–cover–write rather than phonetic approaches to learning.

Mathematics

First, revisiting the left-brain insights at the start of this chapter alongside the current understanding of autism, the following implications for teaching mathematics to children with autism in school and supporting them with school work at home emerge.

Visual Approach

Use a predominantly visual approach introducing numbers and symbols environmentally. Figures 8.1 and 8.2 are useful examples of how this can be achieved.

First	Last
1.	2.

Figure 8.1 A child's first visual schedule, introducing the numbers 1 and 2 with the words first and last.

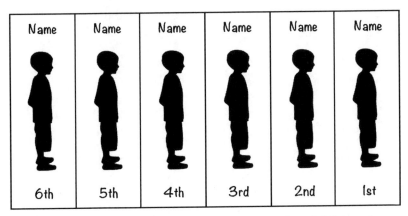

Name	Name	Name	Name	Name	Name
6th	5th	4th	3rd	2nd	1st

Figure 8.2 For situations in school where queuing is beneficial, introduce a visual queuing chart placing and changing names regularly on the representational figures with the ordinal numbers below each figure.[1]

Figures 8.3–8.6 introduce young children with autism to number lines. This should be done as soon as possible, because numbers and counting are essential, intrinsic parts of environments across societies. Numbers are found on cars, buses, mobile phones and many other everyday objects. Sequential numbers are found on houses, apartments, birthday cards, queuing cards and other systems. Carers and professionals use counting to engage and teach children, such as when climbing stairs/steps, playing board games, sharing out treats, counting down activities and so on. However, naming numbers and reciting sequences is not the same as understanding number values and incremental increases and decreases in value. Moreover, this understanding cannot be merely assumed.

One of the easiest places to start with teaching or verifying that a child with autism has this understanding is with a basic number line. Usually the first number line introduced is from 1 to 5. One of the simplest ways to initially imply incremental value is to have a Velcro strip with laminated numbers to attach to it. Eventually number lines are superseded by number squares. Figures 8.3–8.6 are basic examples of number lines and a number square.

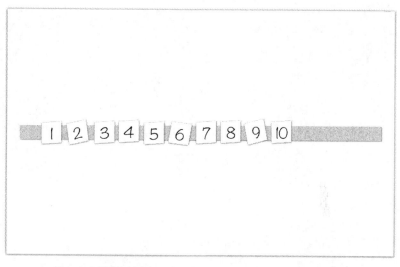

Figure 8.3 A basic number line made with laminated card and Velcro so that numbers can be removed, repositioned and independently sequenced by a child.

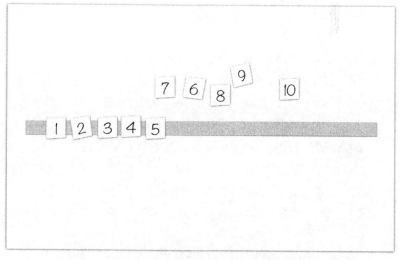

Figure 8.4 A basic number line made with laminated card and Velcro clearly identifying the required sequential task.

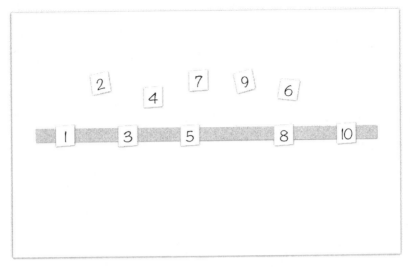

Figure 8.5 A basic number line made with laminated card and Velcro identifying a random ordering task.

1	2	3	4	5	6	7	8	9	10
11	12	13	14	15	16	17	18	19	20
21	22	23	24	25	26	27	28	29	30
31	32	33	34	35	36	37	38	39	40
41	42	43	44	45	46	47	48	49	50
51	52	53	54	55	56	57	58	59	60
61	62	63	64	65	66	67	68	69	70
71	72	73	74	75	76	77	78	79	80
81	82	83	84	85	86	87	88	89	90
91	92	93	94	95	96	97	98	99	100

Figure 8.6 A 'hundred' square made with laminated card and Velcro so that numbers can be removed, repositioned and independently sequenced by a child. It also clearly visually shows the progression and groups/sets of numbers.

Beyond these examples there are numerous ways in which number and symbols can be visually and functionally introduced into the daily life of children with autism. In many ways these are only limited by our imaginations.

While number and symbols are easily introduced into the daily life of young children with autism, the visual approach has long-term relevance. Having read about workplaces that used written instructions to guide and support adults with autism through tasks, in my teaching I used a similar approach with some students. For example, I designed the text sequence and visual aid work-board in Box 8.1 and Figure 8.7 to support recall and practice in addition without carrying using blocks of ten units and single unit cubes.

Box 8.1 A text sequence supporting recall and practice in addition without carrying to be used in conjunction with a visual aid work-board, and blocks of ten units and single unit cubes.

Adding tens and units without carrying
Look at the top number.
Put out the top number's tens.
Put out the top number's units.
Look at the bottom number.
Put out the bottom number's tens.
Put out the bottom number's units.
Put all your units together at the bottom.
Put all your tens next to each other at the bottom.
Count your units and exchange sets of ten for blocks of ten. Put the blocks of ten with the tens. Write the remaining number of units.
Count your tens and write the answer.

Tens and Units Work-Board	
Units	Tens
Answer Total:	

*Figure 8.7 A visual aid work-board made from laminated
card to be used in conjunction with the text in Box 8.1,
with blocks of ten units and single unit cubes.*

Use Personal Interests

The 'self-bound' nature of autism means that the child with autism
will always benefit from materials and equipment that utilise personal
interests. For example, first counting equipment could be objects
of interest, such as Disney characters and little people figures. Also,
materials that feature familiar people and favoured objects aid learning.
For example, when learning to count accurately, photographs of
family and/or class members can prove very successful. Equally, when
learning to do addition and subtraction, using pictures of preferred
items to add or take away with can assist the learning process.

Build from the Concrete to the Abstract and Counter-Check that the Knowable is Rooted in the Doable

All the examples given in Figures 8.1–8.6 are enabling the understanding
and application of numeracy to build from the concretely functional to
the abstract. They are also teaching the knowable while transforming it

to the doable. For example, while Figure 8.2 visually shows children the queuing order of the day or week, it also concretely introduces ordinal numbers, reinforcing values in terms relevant to the child's daily life experiences. This grounding in lived experience is a springboard to the abstract application of ordinal number in later life situations. Situations such as catching trains or buses leaving from the same platform or stop require cognitive, abstract differentiation between the trains or buses arriving at the platform or stop. Moreover, with the visual aid, the child develops a basic knowledge of ordinal numbers and applies this with the appropriate action, that is, taking the correct position in the queue.

Use Repetitious Patterns

Using simple repetitious patterns, gradually introduce more abstract terms and concepts. In other words, allow familiarity to smooth the path to further learning. For example, once a child has shown a sound grasp of number and number values, the next step may be simple addition. When introducing simple addition, it is important to be aware of developing a familiar answer pattern. Transcribe this pattern into simple sequential sentences. Then as the child moves from simple, concrete addition of units to an increasingly complex, abstract calculation, the original pattern is merely updated. Throughout the process, the pattern remains as a visual support/aid.

Use Repetitious Presentation

Especially in the early school years, text and workbooks should have simple, repetitious presentation styles. As with repetitious answer patterns, simple repetitious presentation styles gradually enable more complex designs to be understood and followed. This is important because young children with autism will initially, at least, most likely focus on the visually interesting feature/s on a page. Also, they may not necessarily know where to start/finish work or how to work sequentially through exercises. Clearly some commercially produced schemes have more consistent, clear presentation styles that are more suitable to the needs of young children with autism. Moreover, these can be enhanced with visual guidance techniques, such as writing in green 'Start here' and in red 'Stop here'. As well as or instead of words, shapes and/or lines can be used. Whatever approach is adopted, it must be consistently applied and only gradually changed when/if the need for such indicators diminishes.

Next, applying these insights to the development of the different areas of mathematics, we have clear direction as to the most appropriate approaches and methods to use, especially in the early years.

The Use and Application of Mathematics

Two important aspects of the use and application of mathematics are reasoning and problem-solving. To develop these, the child with autism needs to be taught from the functional to the abstract. Although certain children with autism may visually grasp, recreate and even understand underlining patterns and configurations, rather like the child who reads without understanding, profound use and application of mathematics requires honing in practical tasks and life-applicable problem-solving. Again strategies such as those given previously for the teaching of ordinal number values in child-appropriate situations should be used.

Understanding the language of mathematics is another important aspect of its use and application.[2] Understanding for the child with autism is usually underpinned by functionality. For example, I taught several children with autism who explained environmental objects in terms of their function. Mostly they used descriptive phrases as opposed to nouns, such as 'cuts grass' for lawnmower. Therefore, the basis to understanding the language of number, shape, measurement and so forth is best grounded in knowing concretely the function behind the term/s. Many of the examples given above relating to visual and personalised strategies are based upon this approach.[3]

Another aspect of the use and application of mathematics relates to forms of communication. While the neurotypical human being probably considers language and communication inseparable, relating language predominantly with verbalisation and the written word, the use and application of mathematics seemingly offers different forms of communication. For the child with autism the predominant style of communication in mathematics is visual, with forms that include diagrams, graphs and representational equations. As such, combining the functional and the personal in a daily exposure to visual aids, such as schedules/timetables, may be furthering the development of mathematical skills for children with autism. For example, a child who can decipher the complex schedule shown in Table 8.1 (a similar schedule is illustrated in Chapter 5) has developed the skills necessary to read and follow simple train and bus timetables.

Table 8.1 Table showing a complex weekly schedule/timetable.

Time	Monday	Tuesday	Wednesday	Thursday	Friday
9.00	Break area	Break area	Break area	Break area	Break area
9.10	Work with teacher	Work with teacher	Work with teacher	Work with teacher	Work with teacher
9.30	Greeting	Greeting	Greeting	Greeting	Greeting
10.00	Independent work	Independent work	Independent work	Independent work	Independent work
10.30	Computer	Computer	Computer	Computer	Computer
11.00	Outdoor play	Outdoor play	Outdoor play	Outdoor play	Outdoor play
11.10	Structured play	Structured play	Structured play	Structured play	Structured play
12.00	Group work	Group work	Group work	Group work	Group work
12.15	Exercises	Exercises	Exercises	Exercises	Exercises
12.30	Lunch	Lunch	Lunch	Lunch	Lunch
12.45	Outdoor play	Outdoor play	Outdoor play	Outdoor play	Outdoor play
1.00	Independent work	Independent work	Independent work	Independent work	Independent work
1.30	P.E.	Library	Music	Art and craft	P.E.
2.10	Work with teacher	Work with teacher	Work with teacher	Work with teacher	Work with teacher
2.40	Break area	Break area	Break area	Break area	Break area
3.00	Home	Home	Home	Home	Home

However, another part of the use and application of mathematics requires children to explain their thinking regarding mathematical problems. For some children with autism, giving a verbal explanation or responding to verbal questioning is either problematic or simply impossible. However, there are other ways in which children with autism can show their thinking regarding mathematical problems. These are wide ranging and individual to a child. They include talking to or through puppets and sequentially arranging sentences/photographs/objects to show the process taken. In the case of arranging sentences and/or photographs, the teacher may have observed and recorded in words and/or photographs the child's process to provide the opportunity for these forms of visual explanation. Alternatively, especially with an older or more able child, it can be more probing to present the child with generic sentence and/or photograph/picture sequences.[4] Whatever way is taken to enable a child with autism to fulfil this mathematical requirement, the information gleaned sheds light on the child's understanding of the mathematical problem and its solution. It also illuminates where the child may need to alter or refine her/his thinking.

There is another important outcome to consider, that is, the child with autism is engaging in a relational process.

Shape, Space and Measures

In many ways this area of mathematics may suit the thought processes of children with autism. Shape, space and measures broadly require children to use geometrical properties and relationships in the solution of problems, use computers to create and transform shapes, consider patterns and apply measuring skills contextually. Clearly, these requirements call for visual perception and understanding. Visual perception and understanding can be areas of strength for minds that have a visual learning style.

However, reality does not always marry expectations, and not all children with autism naturally excel in this area of mathematics. There are many reasons why this might be so, but the two most likely reasons are that the child has additional educational need/s or that the minds instructing the child are doing so from a different perspective and style. In the case of the former, an additional educational need is probably the predominant one, and teaching approaches used should be influenced by it. In the case of the latter, I believe that the onus is upon the neurotypical mind to try to accommodate the mind with autism because that endeavour requires relational aspects, such as empathy. Clearly, even while the mind with autism may have the advantage in this area of mathematics, in the arena of relations the neurotypical mind has the advantage.

This advantage is best applied through observation and discussion with all significant persons involved in the child's daily life, as there may be much to be gleaned regarding how a child with autism is already using shape, space and measure in her/his life. For example, there are many children with autism for whom the journey from home to school and back must maintain a regular, unvaried route. These children are familiar with landmarks, turnings, road markings, traffic signals and so forth. Whilst their fixation on a routine journey may be dismissed as rigid thinking, it also gives an insight into how their minds can be developed in this mathematical area. For example, routes can be mapped and modelled allowing a contextual introduction to shape, angles, measures, co-ordinates and so forth.[5] Moreover, the child could be introduced to computers to create and transform landmarks and other features of the route.

Whilst using geometrical properties and relationships to solve problems, using computers to create and transform shapes, considering patterns and applying measuring skills contextually may all be considered areas particularly suited to minds with autism; understanding the language of shape, space and measures is not. As previously stated, understanding for the child with autism is usually underpinned by functionality. Therefore, the language of shape, space and measures requires purposeful, contextual grounding for children with autism. The example given relating to mapping and modelling regular and new routes does exactly that.

Numeracy

As with shape, space and measures, the immediate impression of this area of mathematics is its suitability to minds with autism. Numbers, symbols, sequences, patterns, the operations of number and so forth are heavily visual. So also are the tools and resources that support this area of mathematics. These include the calculators and computers that children are meant to master.

However, this area of mathematics also requires flexible methods of working with number both orally and mentally. It also requires variety in recording calculations, including mental ones. These requirements can be barriers to achievement for children with autism, and should therefore be taken into consideration from the onset of their schooling. In other words, preventative approaches and methods should be employed. These must be visual and functional in nature, using as much as possible repetitious presentation and patterns, personal interests and building from the concrete to the abstract. For example, exploring the number bonds to ten with practical objects or items of personal interest to a child furthers the knowledge that different values amount to the one value: there are different ways to the same end (Table 8.2).

Table 8.2 Exploring the number bonds to ten to be used in conjunction with practical objects, preferably of personal interest to a child, promoting the concept that different values can amount to the same value.

Number bonds to ten	
0 Disney figures + 10 Disney figures = 10 figures $0 + 10 = 10$	10 Disney figures + 0 Disney figures = 10 figures $10 + 0 = 10$
1 Disney figure + 9 Disney figures = 10 figures $1 + 9 = 10$	9 Disney figures + 1 Disney figure = 10 figures $9 + 1 = 10$
2 Disney figures + 8 Disney figures = 10 figures $2 + 8 = 10$	8 Disney figures + 2 Disney figures = 10 figures $8 + 2 = 10$

3 Disney figures + 7 Disney figures = 10 figures 3 + 7 = 10	7 Disney figures + 3 Disney figures = 10 figures 7 + 3 = 10
4 Disney figures + 6 Disney figures = 10 figures 4 + 6 = 10	6 Disney figures + 4 Disney figures = 10 figures 6 + 4 = 10
5 Disney figures + 5 Disney figures = 10 figures 5 + 5 = 10	5 Disney figures + 5 Disney figures = 10 figures 5 + 5 = 10

Another example involves the use of practical resources of personal interest to explore that subtraction is the inverse of addition. This furthers the recognition that there are a variety of methods for adding and subtracting, and promotes the conceptualisation of regularity and sequencing. Table 8.3 is just one way to explore subtraction as the inverse of addition.

Table 8.3 Example of how practical resources of personal interest can be used to explore subtraction as the inverse of addition.

Addition versus subtraction	
10 Lego bricks + 0 Lego bricks = 10 bricks 10 + 0 = 10	10 Lego bricks – 0 Lego bricks = 10 bricks 10 – 0 = 10
10 Lego bricks + 1 Lego brick = 11 bricks 10 + 1 = 11	10 Lego bricks – 1 Lego brick = 9 bricks 10 – 1 = 9
10 Lego bricks + 2 Lego bricks = 12 bricks 10 + 2 = 12	10 Lego bricks – 2 Lego bricks = 8 bricks 10 – 2 = 8
10 Lego bricks + 3 Lego bricks = 13 bricks 10 + 3 = 13	10 Lego bricks – 3 Lego bricks = 7 bricks 10 – 3 = 7
10 Lego bricks + 4 Lego bricks = 14 bricks 10 + 4 = 14	10 Lego bricks – 4 Lego bricks = 6 bricks 10 – 4 = 6

10 Lego bricks + 5 Lego bricks = 15 bricks $10 + 5 = 15$	10 Lego bricks – 5 Lego bricks = 5 bricks $10 - 5 = 5$
10 Lego bricks + 6 Lego bricks = 16 bricks $10 + 6 = 16$	10 Lego bricks – 6 Lego bricks = 4 bricks $10 - 6 = 4$
10 Lego bricks + 7 Lego bricks = 17 bricks $10 + 7 = 17$	10 Lego bricks – 7 Lego bricks = 3 bricks $10 - 7 = 3$
10 Lego bricks + 8 Lego bricks = 18 bricks $10 + 8 = 18$	10 Lego bricks – 8 Lego bricks = 2 bricks $10 - 8 = 2$
10 Lego bricks + 9 Lego bricks = 19 bricks $10 + 9 = 19$	10 Lego bricks – 9 Lego bricks = 1 brick $10 - 9 = 1$
10 Lego bricks + 10 Lego bricks = 20 bricks $10 + 10 = 20$	10 Lego bricks – 10 Lego bricks = 0 bricks $10 - 10 = 0$

With both examples, the verbal child is encouraged to relate the operations to the attending adult. For the non-verbal child, alternative means of expressing his/her working should be found. This may be pre-prepared sentence strips or written explanations.

Handling Data

There are two main areas to handling data that need to be considered. These are (1) collecting, representing and interpreting data and (2) understanding and using probability. Inevitably both areas include acquiring an appropriate vocabulary and discussion.

However, generally, the vocabulary of data and probability has some regularity to it. For example, terms such as 'certain', 'likely' and 'improbable' have consistent, established meanings when discussing experiments and findings. Also, especially in the primary and early secondary school years, the vocabulary predominantly arises from concrete situations/events and predictions. For example, conclusions regarding uncertain and misleading data can be drawn from statistical findings and graphs. Therefore, due to these advantages, the focal teaching points for children with autism become the acquisition and understanding of the vocabulary because, once acquired and understood, a consistent, concrete and predictable application is possible.

As with the use and application of mathematics, acquiring and understanding the vocabulary of handling data is best achieved through materials and resources that combine functionality and visual teaching. Fortunately, this area of mathematics readily lends itself to such as it includes tables, graphs, diagrams and the use of computers to source and represent data.

Also, as noted in Chapter 6, it is important not to equate non-verbalisation with ability or, in this case, lack of acquisition and understanding. For the non-verbal child, alternative means of expressing these should be sought and found. This may be in the form of labels, pre-prepared sentence strips, word processing or written explanations. In my experience, the non-verbal child with autism can be limited by our creative ability to provide a child-appropriate means of expression. Moreover, as the means must suit the task or problem, finding one means and rigidly sticking to it with a child may lead to frustration for both the child and the teacher. It may also lead to an incorrect assessment of the child's knowledge and understanding. So, be creative and adaptive towards both the child and the process.

Notes

1. It is also a welcome addition to place photographs of the children's faces on the heads of the figures, although this may initially look odd as the silhouettes are conveying a left-to-right, side-of-face viewpoint. However, with the young child with autism, this is enabling both word and person recognition.
2. The understanding of the language of mathematics extends to the appropriate usage of numerals and other mathematical symbols.
3. The concrete understanding of comparative and relational terms comes under the umbrella of the functional approach. These terms include size and position, such as 'the biggest' and 'behind'.
4. The use of generic sequences may also expose the child to possible different approaches to mathematical problems, which is another significant part of this aspect of mathematics.

5. This is also a way to introduce alternative routes to a child with autism who has developed rigid thinking regarding routes taken. Rather like a Social Story™, the mapping/modelling of alternative routes can rehearse the child, making the unfamiliar acceptable and possibly fun. Photographs of the new route's landmarks and other features can be taken and used to assist the mapping/modelling process. The old route and the new route can be visually shown side by side with the same departure and arrival points emphasised. It is important not to rush the preparation and for the child to have a map of the journey to be taken with him/her when it is attempted.

Conclusion

WHAT NEXT?

From the perspective of more than 30 years of educational service and passionate enquiry, in this book I have outlined the major historical constructions of autism from which many of our present interventions and practices evolved. In doing so I expanded upon current understanding and practice regarding the care and education of children with autism with the intention of enabling the reader to develop critical insights into what they read and hear, and how they behave and respond towards people with autism. Ultimately, I hope that the content of this book enables greater informed choices between educational methods and approaches for individual children with autism.

I also considered some of the controversial issues regarding how we construct disorders, impairments and difference. I argued that these are dependent upon socio-cultural mindsets and underpinning theoretical assumptions. Overall, my aim in doing so was to propose that autism should be viewed as a different way of seeing and being in the world.

Moreover, with the perspective of autism as difference rather than impairment, I challenged the common belief that autism is increasingly prevalent. To do so I outlined several reasons why changes in society and constructions of the child and childhood may have nurtured characteristics and behaviours we relate with autism. Then, from these explanations, I proposed the need for an alternative pedagogy that understands and respects autism. This pedagogy challenges many of our current theories of educational 'good practice', particularly the collaborative, language-rich learning environment now enjoyed by many, but usually distressing and stressful to those with autism.

In this brief conclusion I draw many of these ideas together to consider the possible future of people with autism within our changing society. My starting place is the line of thought that autism may be the next stage in humanity's evolution. I first heard this suggested nearly 20 years ago, by an educational psychologist at a workshop for parents of children with Asperger's syndrome (AS). At the time I found the thought disturbing, imagining a world in which empathy and social interaction would be sparing aberrations.

However, time has better informed my opinion.

In my lifetime most of humanity's innovations have been technological. Generally, these have been created by minds that Baron-Cohen (2009a) in his empathy–systemising theory (E–S theory) would see as being strongly weighted towards systems rather than empathy. This theory was touched upon in Chapters 1, 2 and 4. However, here it warrants further elaboration because, as we navigate through the changes new ideas regarding autism require, theories that focus on strengths and learning styles as much as aberrations are needed to illuminate our path. In other words, as we review our current constructions, beliefs and opinions of autism, we may need theories and ideas that bolster a new perspective of difference. For me, Baron-Cohen's (2009a, 2009b) E–S theory does exactly that.

The E–S theory is not confined to delays and deficits, as it names and expounds 'areas of strength by reference to intact or even superior skills in systemizing' (Baron-Cohen 2009b, p.6):

> According to the empathizing–systemizing (E–S) theory, autism and Asperger syndrome are best explained not just with reference to empathy (below average) but also with reference to a second psychological factor (systemizing), which is either average or even above average. So it is the discrepancy between E and S that determines if you are likely to develop an autism spectrum condition. (Baron-Cohen 2009b, p.7)

For example, Baron-Cohen's definition of systemising as 'the drive to analyse or construct systems' (2009b, p.7), coupled with his description of systems as rule-followers, offers a positive explanation of the need for routines and rigidity of thinking. Baron-Cohen (2009a, p.71) outlines that 'when we are trying to identify the rules that govern' a system we do so 'to predict how the system will behave'. Also, he names different types of systems. These include 'mechanical systems (e.g., a video-recorder), numerical systems (e.g., a train timetable), abstract systems (e.g., the syntax of a language)' and 'natural systems (e.g., tidal wave patterns)'. While predicting how mechanical, numerical, abstract and natural systems will behave is doable, predicting how people will behave is not, and clearly this is the essential dilemma for persons whose minds are systems weighted. However, from a psychological perspective, the drive to predict the latter makes absolute sense, because if we could predict how people will behave we could avoid stress and distress. Therefore, if the need for routines and rigidity of thinking is understood as a by-product of minds driven to identify the rules that govern systems to make workable predictions, psychologically these traits make sense and are positively reframed.

Moreover, evidence of systemising tendencies in children with autism can be found in several studies. These include a study by Baron-Cohen *et al.* (2001) in which children with AS aged between 8 and 11 years scored higher than an older comparison group on a physics test. Also, they include studies using the 'Systemizing Quotient' (SQ) designed by Baron-Cohen and colleagues for use with children with AS and high-functioning autism.[1] One such study found that these children score higher on the SQ than the general population (Baron-Cohen *et al.* 2003). Furthermore, while the SQ is not designed for children with classical autism, there are studies cited as providing evidence of intact or strong systemising ability in this group. These include studies working out how a Polaroid camera works (Baron-Cohen *et al.* 1985; Perner *et al.* 1989), and a study that found better visual sequential skills using physical-causal concepts than a control group of peers (Baron-Cohen, Leslie and Frith 1986).

Nevertheless, the E–S theory is not without critics. Criticism has been directed at its focus on persons with AS or high-functioning autism. Also, the Connellan *et al.* (2000) study, upon which this theory rests, has been contested. This study found that male neonates looked longer at objects, and female neonates looked longer at people. However, a review of studies into infant perception by Spelke (2005, p.952) concluded that while 'most studies find no sex differences... Some studies find an advantage for female infants, particularly in the domains of mechanical reasoning and the ages at which new abilities emerge.'

For me, the issue with the theory is more to do with common sense than academics. Commonly within academia, once a theory has been conceived, research to support or refute it is spawned. In terms of support, what this may mean is that we may be finding what we have gone looking for.

Nevertheless, despite this and the academic criticisms voiced, I still glimpse in the E–S theory some illumination of a very long tunnel. The creations and inventions of minds capable of the impressive technological advances I have witnessed in my lifetime, be they male or female brains, clearly have a bias for systems without decrying their empathetic capabilities. So, while we may argue about issues such as sex differences and the ratios of those in the information technology industry with or without autism, what I can find no disagreement upon is the propensity for systemising experienced by those with autism. Moreover, the influence of these technological advances upon the minds of children, be they with or without autism, has, in my opinion, reached an omnipotence over the older, more traditional spheres of influence I grew up with, such as family and church. Also, where spheres of influence in my youth generally had demarcated environments, information technology knows no borders. We find it in every setting, including our homes, schools, workplaces, cafes and public transport facilities.

Therefore, I contend that the acceleration of technological progress makes our understanding of autism as difference a necessity. As outlined in Chapter 4, the technological world we now inhabit increasingly fuels thinking and characteristics we could consider to be 'autistic'. It is highly possible with the growth in information technology, and changes in how we communicate and access social interaction, that some of those we now consider the neurotypicals may in the future be classified as those with impairments and disorders – perhaps impairments and disorders of an excessive empathetic nature. If AS, high-functioning autism or mild autism equal the next stage of evolution, surely it would be in our own interest to educate individuals so labelled according to their strengths rather than their weaknesses, lest they in some tomorrow world try to 'cure' us of our diseases.

However, in concluding I also wish to challenge those who isolate AS, high-functioning autism or mild autism as the chosen subset of the evolutionary gifted within the autism umbrella group. I have even heard some proponents of this belief search through the pages of history declaring persons of renown as persons with AS. With little more than anecdotal evidence and austere or idiosyncratic photographs, they list off person after person of repute with the conviction that because they showed this or that trait they are/were clearly a person with AS. It is not that I dispute all the claims being made. Sometimes I feel the urge to agree with the diagnosis being pronounced. My dislike of this rests with (1) the arrogance of assessing and diagnosing another human being on little information, no face-to-face interaction and without the consent of the person if alive or any living family member if deceased, and (2) the creation of yet another 'them' and 'us' divide that for some may imply that, while 'us' are gifted, 'them' are impaired. For me, this thinking is detrimental to the way forward, which is a total recognition that the whole group of persons with autism think differently from the neurotypicals. Surely that is enough 'them' and 'us' without subdividing a group already set apart by the dominant 'us' in current society?

Therefore, for me, 'What next?' has three features. The first is the vision of autism as a different way of perceiving and relating to the external world rather than a disorder or an impairment, the second is a pedagogy designed around the strengths of minds with autism that clearly hear a different drumbeat, and the third is that this vision and the pedagogy it generates will eliminate fractures and demarcations between those living with an ASD or with someone with an ASD.

Note

1. Both the 'Empathy Quotient' and the 'Systemizing Quotient' can be found in the appendices of Baron-Cohen's book *Zero Degrees of Empathy* (2011).

Further Reading

I was often asked by teachers, workers and parents to recommend some good reading matter about autism. Quite simply looking for a book to read on autism can be very daunting. There is a vast number of books and many have a bias towards one type of approach or intervention. Therefore, for me, some of the most invaluable books about autism have been written by people with autism. Their autobiographies, stories and accounts are the greatest source of pertinent information and insight in this field. Although there are many books of this nature, I strongly recommend that Patricia Howlin's *Autism and Asperger Syndrome: Preparing for Adulthood* written in conjunction with Ros Blackburn (2004 [1997]), Jasmine Lee O'Neill's *Through the Eyes of Aliens* (2000), Donna Williams's *Nobody Nowhere* (1998 [1992]) and the plethora of books written by Temple Grandin (2006, 2012, 2013, 2015a and b) are placed on everyone's reading lists.

References

American Psychiatric Association (2013) *Diagnostic and Statistical Manual of Mental Disorders, Fifth Edition.* Arlington, VA: American Psychiatric Publishing.

Andrews, N., Miller, E., Grant, A., Stowe, J., Osborne, V. and Taylor, B. (2004) 'Thimerosal exposure in infants and developmental disorders: a retrospective cohort study in the United Kingdom does not support a causal association.' *Pediatrics 114*, 3, 584–591.

Ayres, A. J. and Robbins, J. (1979) *Sensory Integration and the Child.* Torrance, CA: Western Psychological Services.

Baron-Cohen, S. (2003) *The Essential Difference: Male and Female Brains and the Truth about Autism.* New York: Basic Books.

Baron-Cohen, S. (2009a) 'Autism: the empathizing–systemizing (E–S) theory.' *Annals of the New York Academy of Sciences 1156* (The Year in Cognitive Neuroscience 2009), 68–80.

Baron-Cohen, S. (2009b) *The Empathizing–Systemizing (E–S) Theory of Autism: Implications for Education.* Cambridge: University of Cambridge, Autism Research Centre, Departments of Experimental Psychology and Psychiatry. Accessed on 15/11/2017 at www.neuroscience.cam.ac.uk/publications/download.php?id=40523.

Baron-Cohen, S. (2010) 'Conference address.' Seeing the Light Conference (presented by Research Autism, UK), London, 2 November.

Baron-Cohen, S. (2011) *Zero Degrees of Empathy: A New Theory of Human Cruelty.* London: Allen Lane/Penguin Books.

Baron-Cohen, S. (2012) 'Autism spectrum disorder (ASD) vs. autism spectrum condition (ASC): is one small letter important?' Paper given at The Research Autism Conference: Disorder or Difference? Autistic Experiences of School and Beyond, London, 14 November.

Baron-Cohen, S. and Hammer, J. (1997) 'Is autism an extreme form of the male brain?' *Advances in Infancy Research 11*, 193–217.

Baron-Cohen, S., Leslie, A. M. and Frith, U. (1985) 'Does the autistic child have a "theory of mind"?' *Cognition 21*, 37–46. Accessed on 15/11/2017 at www.researchgate.net/publication/20222469_Does_the_Autistic_Child_Have_a_Theory_of_Mind.

Baron-Cohen, S., Leslie, A. M. and Frith, U. (1986) 'Mechanical, behavioural and intentional understanding of picture stories in autistic children.' *British Journal of Developmental Psychology 4*, 113–125. Accessed on 15/11/2017 at http://docs. autismresearchcentre.com/papers/1986_BC_etal_PictureStoriesInASChildren. pdf.

Baron-Cohen, S., Richler, J., Bisarya, D., Gurunathan, N. and Wheelwright, S. (2003) *The Systemizing Quotient: An Investigation of Adults with Asperger Syndrome or High-Functioning Autism, and Normal Sex Differences.* Cambridge: University of Cambridge, Autism Research Centre, Departments of Experimental Psychology and Psychiatry. Accessed on 15/11/2017 at http://docs.autismresearchcentre. com/papers/2003_BCetal_sysquoAS.pdf.

Baron-Cohen, S., Ring, H., Bullmore, E., Wheelwright, S., Ashwin, C. and Williams, S. (2000) 'The amygdala theory of autism.' *Neuroscience and Behavioural Reviews 24*, 355–364.

Baron-Cohen, S., Wheelwright, S., Spong, A., Scahill, V. and Lawson, J. (2001) *Studies of Theory of Mind: Are Intuitive Physics and Intuitive Psychology Independent?* Cambridge: University of Cambridge, Autism Research Centre, Departments of Experimental Psychology and Psychiatry. Accessed on 15/11/2017 at http:// docs.autismresearchcentre.com/papers/2001_BCetal_kidseyes.pdf.

Bernard, S., Enayati, A., Binstock, T., Roger, H., Redwood, L. and McGinnis, W. (2000) *Autism: A Unique Type of Mercury Poisoning.* Safe Minds. Accessed on 15/11/2017 at https://worldmercuryproject.org/wp-content/uploads/2016/10/Autism_ Unique_-Type_-of_-Mercury_-Poisoning.pdf.

Bettelheim, B. (1967) *The Empty Fortress: Infantile Autism and the Birth of the Self.* New York: Free Press.

Blackburn, R. (2010) 'Logically illogical.' Conference at Letterkenny, Donegal, October.

Bruner, J. (1975) 'The ontogenesis of speech acts.' *Journal of Child Language 2*, 1–19.

Cantwell, D. P. and Baker, L. (1984) 'Research Concerning Families of Children with Autism.' In E. Schopler and G. B. Mesibov (eds) *The Effects of Autism on the Family.* New York: Plenum Press.

Christie, P. (1985) 'Education in school for autistic children: 'What's so special about autism?' Paper given at Nottingham University, 27 April.

Christie, P. (2010) 'Promoting emotional wellbeing in pupils with ASD.' Seminar, Centre for Autism, Middletown, Ireland, 18–19 October.

Clancy, H. and McBride, G. M. (1969) 'The autistic process and its treatment.' *Journal of Child Psychology and Psychiatry 10*, 233–244.

Clark, P. and Rutter, M. (1981) 'Autistic children's responses to structure and to interpersonal demands.' *Journal of Autism and Developmental Disorders 11*, 2, 201–217.

Connellan, J., Baron-Cohen, S., Wheelwright, S., Batki, A. and Ahluwalia, J. (2000) 'Sex differences in human neonatal social perception.' *Infant Behavior and Development 23*, 113–118. Accessed on 15/11/2017 at www.math.kth.se/ matstat/gru/5b1501/F/sex.pdf.

Davis, P. S. (2006) *The Son-Rise Program: A Case Study of a Family Living with Autism.* Accessed on 15/11/2017 at www.autismtreatmentcenter.org/media/pdf/ davis2007.pdf.

De Angelis, M., Piccolo, M., Vannini, L., Siragusa, A., *et al.* (2013) 'Fecal microbiota and metabolome of children with autism and pervasive developmental disorder not otherwise specified.' *PLOS ONE*, 9 October. Accessed on 15/11/2017 at http://journals.plos.org/plosone/article?id=10.1371/journal.pone.0076993.

DeMyer, M. K. (1979) *Parents and Children in Autism.* New York: Wiley.

Dennison, P. E. and Dennison, G. E. (1994) *Brain Gym: Teacher's Edition Revised.* Ventura, CA: Edu-Kinesthetics. (Originally published 1989.)

Dewey, J. (1930) *Democracy and Education: An Introduction to the Philosophy of Education.* New York: Macmillan. (Originally published 1916.) Accessed on 15/11/2017 at https://en.wikisource.org/wiki/Democracy_and_Education.

Di Pellegrino, G., Fadiga, L., Fogassi, L., Gallese, V. and Rizzolatti, G. (1992) 'Understanding motor events: a neurophysiological study.' *Experimental Brain Research 91*, 176–180. Accessed on 15/11/2017 at www.uni-muenster. de/imperia/md/content/psyifp/aeechterhoff/wintersemester2011-12/ vorlesungkommperskonflikt/dipellegrino_etal_understmotorevents_ebr1992. pdf.

Doshi-Velez, F., Avillach, P., Palmer, N., Bousvaros, A., *et al.* (2015) 'Prevalence of inflammatory bowel disease among patients with autism spectrum disorders.' *Inflammatory Bowel Diseases 21*, 10, 2281–2288. Accessed on 15/11/2017 at www.ncbi.nlm.nih.gov/pubmed/26218138.

Ecclestone, K. and Hayes, D. (2008) *The Dangerous Rise of Therapeutic Education.* London: Routledge.

Ecker, C. (2010) 'Can biology help to facilitate the diagnosis of autism spectrum disorder?' Research Autism Wing Conference Paper, November.

Ephraim, G. W. E. (1979) 'Developmental Processes in Mental Handicap: A Generative Structure Approach.' Unpublished PhD thesis, Brunel University, Department of Psychology.

Finegold, S. M., Dowd, S. E., Gontcharova, V., Liu, C., *et al.* (2010) 'Pyrosequencing study of fecal microflora of autistic and control children.' *Anaerobe 16*, 4, 444–453.

Finegold, S. M., Molitoris, D., Song, Y., Liu, C., *et al.* (2002) 'Gastrointestinal microflora studies in late-onset autism.' *Clinical Infectious Diseases 35*, 1, 6–16.

Folstein, S. E. and Rutter, M. (1978) 'Infantile autism: a genetic study of 21 twin pairs.' *Journal of Child Psychology and Psychiatry 18*, 297–321.

Fombonne, E., Zakarian, R., Bennett, L., Meng, L. and MacClean-Heywood, D. (2006) 'Pervasive developmental disorders in Montreal, Quebec, Canada: prevalence and links with immunizations.' *Pediatrics 118*, 1, 139–150.

Foucault, M. (2006) *History of Madness.* London: Routledge. (Originally published 1961.)

Frost, L. and Bondy, A. (2002) *The Picture Exchange Communication System: Training Manual*, 2nd edition. Brighton: Pyramid Educational Consultants.

Furedi, F. (2003) *Therapy Culture: Cultivating Vulnerability in an Uncertain Age.* London: Routledge.

Geschwind, N. and Galaburda, A. M. (1987) *Cerebral Lateralization: Biological Mechanisms, Associations and Pathology.* Cambridge, MA: MIT Press.

Goddard, S. (1996) *A Teacher's Window into the Child's Mind and Papers from The Institute for Neuro-Physiological Psychology: A Non-Invasive Approach to Solving Learning and Behavior Problems.* Eugene, OR: Fern Ridge Press.

Goines, P. and Van der Water, J. (2010) 'The immune system's role in the biology of autism.' *Current Opinion in Neurology 23,* 2, 111–117. Accessed on 15/11/2017 at www.ncbi.nlm.nih.gov/pmc/articles/PMC2898160.

Goldfarb, W. (1961) *Childhood Schizophrenia.* Cambridge, MA: Harvard University Press.

Government of Ireland (2001) *Educational Provision and Support for Persons with Autistic Spectrum Disorders: The Report of the Task Force on Autism.* Dublin: SESS. Accessed on 15/11/2017 at www.sess.ie/sites/default/files/Autism%20Task%20Force%20Report.pdf.

Grandin. T. (2006) *Thinking in Pictures: And Other Reports from My Life with Autism.* London: Bloomsbury.

Grandin. T. (2012) *Different Not Less: Inspiring Stories of Achievement and Successful Employment from Adults with Autism, Asperger's and ADHD.* Arlington, TX: Future Horizons.

Grandin. T. and Paneck, R. (2013) *The Autistic Brain: Helping Different Kinds of Mind Succeed.* New York: Houghton Mifflin Harcourt.

Grandin. T. (2015a) *Temple Talks About Autism and Sensory Issues: The World's Leading Expert on Autism Shares Her Advice and Experience.* Arlington, TX: Future Horizons.

Grandin. T. (2015b) *The Way I See It: A Personal Look at Autism and Asperger's. Revised and Expanded.* Arlington, TX: Future Horizons.

Gray, C. (1994a) *The New Social Story Book.* Arlington, VA: Future Horizons.

Gray, C. (1994b) *Comic Strip Conversations.* Arlington, VA: Future Horizons.

Greenspan, S. (1979) *Intelligence and Adaptation: An Integration of Psychoanalytic and Piagetian Developmental Psychology.* New York: International Universities Press.

Greenspan, S. and Salmon, J. (1995) *The Challenging Child: Understanding, Raising and Enjoying the Five 'Difficult' Types of Children.* Cambridge, MA: Perseus Books.

Greenspan, S. and Wieder, S. (1997) *The Child with Special Needs: Encouraging Intellectual and Emotional Growth.* Cambridge, MA: Perseus Books.

Greenspan, S. and Wieder, S. (2003) 'Climbing the symbolic ladder in the DIR model through Floortime/interactive play.' *Autism 7,* 4, 425–435.

Hardyment, C. (1992) 'Looking at Children: A History of Childhood 1600 to the Present.' In S. Holdsworth and J. Crossley (eds) *Innocence and Experience: Images of Children in British Art from 1600 to the Present.* Manchester: Manchester City Art Galleries.

Harvey, C. (2015) 'Living Legacies: Valuing Lives of Service.' Education doctorate thesis, Liverpool Hope University.

Health Canada (1997) *The Safety of Dental Amalgam.* Ottawa: Minister of Health.

Hermelin, B. (2001) *Bright Splinters of the Mind: A Personal Story of Research with Autistic Savants.* London: Jessica Kingsley Publishers.

Hermelin, B. and O'Connor, N. (1970) *Psychological Experiments with Autistic Children.* Oxford: Pergamon Press.

Housden, M. (2002) *Hannah's Gift: Lessons from a Life Fully Lived.* New York: HarperCollins.

Howlin, P. (2004) *Autism and Asperger Syndrome: Preparing for Adulthood.* (Foreword by R. Blackburn.) Abingdon: Routledge. (Originally published 1997.)

Hsiao, E. Y., McBride, S. W., Hsien, S., Sharon, G., *et al.* (2013) 'The microbiota modulates gut physiological and behavioural abnormalities associated with neurodevelopmental disorders.' *Cell 155*, 7, 1451–1463. Accessed on 15/11/2017 at www.cell.com/cell/pdf/S0092-8674(13)01473-6.pdf.

Hviid, A., Stellfeld, M., Wohlfahrt, J. and Melbye, M. (2003) 'Association between thimerosal-containing vaccine and autism.' *Journal of the American Medical Association 290*, 13, 1763–1766.

Jain, A., Marshall, J., Buikema, A., Bancroft, T., Kelly, J. P. and Newschaffer, C. J. (2015) 'Autism occurrence by MMR vaccine status among US children with older siblings with and without autism.' *Journal of the American Medical Association 313*, 15, 1534–1540.

Kanner, L. (1943) 'Autistic disturbances of affective contact.' *Nervous Child 2*, 217–250. Accessed on 15/11/2017 at www.neurodiversity.com/library_kanner_1943.pdf.

Kim, Y. S., Fombonne, E., Koh, Y. J., Kim, S. J., Cheon, K. A. and Leventhal, B. L. (2014) 'A comparison of DSM-IV pervasive developmental disorder and DSM-5 autism spectrum disorder prevalence in an epidemiologic sample.' *Journal of the American Academy of Child and Adolescent Psychiatry 53*, 5, 500–508.

Løvaas, O. I. (1987) 'Behavioural treatment and normal educational and intellectual functioning in young autistic children.' *Journal of Consulting and Clinical Psychology 55*, 1, 3–9. Accessed on 15/11/2017 at www.beca-aba.com/articles-and-forms/lovaas-1987.pdf.

Lucarelli, S., Frediani, T., Zingoni, A. M., Ferruzzi, F., *et al.* (1995) 'Food allergy and infantile autism.' *Panminerva Medica 37*, 3, 137–141.

MacLean, P. D. (1952) 'Some psychiatric implications of physiological studies on frontotemporal portion of limbic system (visceral brain).' *Electroencephalography and Clinic Neurophysiology 4*, 4, 407–418.

Mandavilli, A. (2016) 'How "shock therapy" is saving some children with autism: electroconvulsive therapy is far more beneficial – and banal – than its torturous reputation suggests.' *The Atlantic*, 27 October. Accessed on 15/11/2017 at www.theatlantic.com/health/archive/2016/10/how-shock-therapy-is-saving-some-children-with-autism/505448.

McAdoo, W. G. and DeMyer, M. K. (1978) 'Personality Characteristics of Parents.' In M. Rutter and E. Schopler (eds) *Autism: A Reappraisal of Concepts and Treatment.* New York: Plenum Press.

Molloy, C., Morrow, A., Meinzen-Derr, J., Schleifer, K., *et al.* (2006) 'Elevated cytokine levels in children with autism spectrum disorder.' *Journal of Neuroimmunology 172*, 198–205.

Moloney, P. (2010) 'How can a chord be weird if it expresses your soul? Some critical reflections on the diagnosis of Aspergers syndrome.' *Disability and Society 25*, 2, 135–148.

National Autism Center (NAC) (2015) *Findings and Conclusions: National Standards Project (Phase 2).* Randolph, MA: NAC.

National Institute of Neurological Disorders and Stroke (NINDS) (2014) *Post-Stroke Rehabilitation 14*, 1846. Washington, DC: National Institutes of Health.

Nind, M. and Hewett, D. (1998) *Access to Communication: Developing the Basics of Communication with People with Severe Learning Difficulties through Intensive Interaction.* London: David Fulton. (Originally published 1994.)

O'Neill, J. L. (2000) *Through the Eyes of Aliens: A Book about Autistic People.* London: Jessica Kingsley Publishers.

Parracho, H. M., Bingham, M. O., Gibson, G. R. and McCartney, A. L. (2005) 'Differences between the gut microflora of children with autistic spectrum disorders and that of healthy children.' *Journal of Medical Microbiology 54*, 10, 987–991.

Perner, J., Frith, U., Leslie, A. M. and Leekam, S. (1989) 'Exploration of the autistic child's theory of mind: knowledge, belief, and communication.' *Child Development 60*, 689–700.

Pinney, R. (1983) *Bobby: Breakthrough of an Autistic Child.* London: Harvill Press.

Pinney, R. (1994) *Special Times: Listening to Children, Children's Hours Trust.* East Marden, West Sussex: Children's Hours Trust. (Originally published 1993 by Rachel Pinney, Philip Carr-Gomm and Meg Robinson.)

Premack, D. and Woodruff, G. (1978) 'Does the chimpanzee have a theory of mind?' *Behavioural and Brain Sciences 4*, 4, 515–526.

Price, C. S., Thompson, W. W., Goodson, B., Weintraub, E. S., *et al.* (2010) 'Prenatal and infant exposure to thimerosal from vaccines and immunoglobulins and risk of autism.' *Pediatrics 126*, 4, 656–664.

Richer, J. (1978) 'The Partial Non-Communication of Culture to Autistic Children – An Application of Human Ethology.' In M. Rutter and E. Schopler (eds) *Autism: A Reappraisal of Concepts and Treatment.* New York: Plenum Press.

Richer, J. (1983) 'Development of Social Avoidance in Autistic Children.' In A. Oliverio and M. Zappella (eds) *The Behaviour of Human Infants.* New York: Plenum Press.

Richet, C. (1913) 'Nobel Lecture: Anaphylaxis.' Accessed on 15/11/2017 at www.nobelprize.org/nobel_prizes/medicine/laureates/1913/richet-lecture.html.

Rimland, B. (1978) 'Savant Capabilities of Autistic Children and Their Cognitive Implications.' In G. Serban (ed.) *Cognitive Defects in the Development of Mental Illness.* New York: Brunner/Mazel.

Roth, I. (1990) 'Autism.' In I. Roth (ed.) *Introduction to Psychology: Volume 2.* Milton Keynes: Open University Press.

Ryan, S. (2010) 'Meltdowns, surveillance and managing emotions: going out with children with autism.' *Healthplace 16*, 5, 868–875. Accessed on 15/11/2017 at www.ncbi.nlm.nih.gov/pmc/articles/PMC2927009.

Sacks, O. (1985) *The Man Who Mistook His Wife for a Hat: And Other Clinical Tales.* London: Gerald Duckworth.

Saloviita, T., Ruusila, L. and Ruusila, U. (2000) 'Incidence of savant syndrome in Finland.' *Perceptual and Motor Skills 91*, 120–122.

Santayana, G. (1905) *The Life of Reason or The Phases of Human Progress.* New York: C. Scribner's and Sons.

Schechter, R. and Grether, J. K. (2008) 'Continuing increases in autism reported to California's developmental services system: mercury in retrograde.' *Archives of General Psychiatry 65*, 1, 19–24.

Sennett, R. (1998) *The Corrosion of Character: The Personal Consequences of Work in the New Capitalism.* New York: W. W. Norton.

Shic, F., Macari, S. and Chawarska, K. (2014) 'Speech disturbs face scanning in 6-month olds who develop autism spectrum disorder.' *Biological Psychiatry 75*, 3, 231–237.

Silberman, S. (2015) *Neurotribes: The Legacy of Autism and How to Think Smarter about People Who Think Differently.* Sydney: Allen and Unwin.

Skare, I. (1995) 'Mass balance and systematic uptake of mercury released from dental amalgam fillings.' *Water, Air and Soil Pollution 80*, 1, 59–67.

Skinner, B. F. (1957) *Verbal Behavior.* Acton, MA: Copley Publishing Group.

Spelke, E. S. (2005) 'Sex differences in intrinsic aptitude for mathematics and science? A critical review.' *American Psychologist 60*, 9, 950–958. Accessed on 15/11/2017 at http://harvardlds.org/wp-content/uploads/2017/01/spelke2005-1.pdf.

Thompson, W. W., Price, C., Goodson, B., Shay, D. K., *et al.* (2007) 'Early thimerosal exposure and neuropsychological outcomes at 7 to 10 years.' *New England Journal of Medicine 357*, 1281–1292.

Tinbergen, N. and Tinbergen, E. (1983) *'Autistic' Children: New Hope for a Cure.* London: Allen and Unwin. Accessed on 15/11/2017 at www.ticinoinforna.com/autistic-children-new-hope-for-a-cure.pdf.

Wachtel, L. E., Kahng, S. W., Dhossche, D. M., Cascella, N. and Reti, I. M. (2008) 'ECT for catatonia in an autistic girl.' *American Journal of Psychiatry 165*, 3, 329–333. Accessed on 15/11/2017 at http://ajp.psychiatryonline.org/doi/abs/10.1176/appi.ajp.2007.07081246.

Wakefield, A. J., Murch, S. H., Anthony, A., Linnell, J., *et al.* (1998) 'Ileal-lymphoid-nodular hyperplasia, non-specific colitis, and pervasive developmental disorder in children.' *Lancet 351*, 9103, 637–641. (Article now retracted by authors.)

Williams, D. (1998) *Nobody Nowhere.* New York: Avon Books. (Originally published 1992.)

Williams, K. R. and Wishart, J. G. (2003) 'The Son-Rise Program intervention for autism: an investigation into family experiences.' *Journal of Intellectual Disability Research 47*, Parts 4–5, 291–299.

Wing, L. and Gould, J. (1979) 'Severe impairments of social interaction and associated abnormalities in children: epidemiology and classification.' *Journal of Autism and Developmental Disorders 9*, 11–29.

World Health Organization (2003) *Elemental Mercury and Inorganic Mercury Compounds: Human Health Aspects.* Geneva: WHO (United Nations Environment Programme, International Labour Organization and World Health Organization within the framework of the Inter-Organization Programme for the Sound Management of Chemicals). Accessed on 15/11/2017 at www.who.int/ipcs/publications/cicad/en/cicad50.pdf.

World Health Organization (2008) 'No vaccine for the scaremongers.' *Bulletin of the World Health Organization 86*, 6, 417–496. Accessed on 15/11/2017 at www.who.int/bulletin/volumes/86/6/08-030608.pdf?ua=1.

Subject Index

Author Index